coins
here

Your Dreamy Days adventure is complete!

We hope you loved exploring these beautiful,
whimsical scenes filled with cows, frogs, bear,
bunnies, ducks, and otters! This book w
designed to bring a little magic and relaxation i
your day.

We'd love to see your dreamy creations! Tag u
@theCoolKitschClub on Instagram and TikTok
share your artwork with the world!

If these sweet, peaceful moments made you s
please leave us a review and help spread the dre
vibes!

Printed in Great Britain
by Amazon

59407327R00037

Revision Notes & Sample Essays

Shakespeare's
Julius Caesar

Daisy de Souza

LOL SERIES

For

Amelie, Aurelia and Anya

With Love

Author: Daisy de Souza

ISBN:9781981059690

Contents

PREFACE

This study guide is intended for students in High/Secondary School revising Shakespeare's *Julius Caesar* for the GCSE English Literature paper and other equivalent examinations. It provides a comment on each scene in the play, notes on themes and characters, as well as sample answers to context and essay questions. The sample answers specifically address questions and help students focus on providing relevant information in their own answers.

The material in this book gives ONE interpretation of the play, and notes and sample answers should not be learnt by rote and regurgitated in the examination. Instead, you are encouraged to study the play closely and develop your own responses to characters and incidents. Besides expecting detailed knowledge of the book, examiners look for personal insights from students. Remember your ideas need to be supported with evidence from the text. Therefore, no matter how you consider it, the textbook is your most important book. No study guide can ever be a substitute for it.

INTRODUCTION TO THE PLAY

Julius Caesar was written in 1599 and published in 1623. Shakespeare's source for his play was Sir Thomas North's translation of Plutarch's *Lives of the Noble Grecians and Romans*, which provided him with the outline of the plot, including accounts of minor incidents, and material for the appearances and personalities of his characters, especially Caesar, Brutus and Antony. However, Shakespeare selected details, altering or expanding the original accounts, so that scenes come dramatically to life. The characters, including the less significant ones, have become more human and individual and the final creations are really Shakespeare's own.

Historical Background

As a tragedy, *Julius Caesar* has a well-known historical basis. In 60 B.C., Caesar, Pompey and Crassus formed the first Triumvirate, a coalition of three men who governed Rome in defiance of the Senate. Between 58-50 B.C. Caesar conquered Gaul and at the same time improved his political position in Rome. Pompey became restive toward Caesar as did Crassus toward him. Crassus was killed in the battle against the Parthians in 53 B.C. but relations did not improve between Caesar and Pompey. The breach came soon and Pompey became the champion of the Senate in the civil war that followed. Caesar crushed Pompey's army in Spain before defeating him at Pharsalus in 48 B.C. He then pursued him from Thessaly to Egypt, where he was murdered. Brutus and Cassius were supporters of Pompey, but Caesar forgave them, as he did all of his opponents, and gave many of them responsible positions in his new regime. When Caesar defeated Pompey's sons, he seemed to have consolidated his position as the most powerful man in Rome. He had the power to appoint officers of the state and was given several honours. Statues of Caesar were erected in the Capitol. Caesar was increasingly ruling Rome like a monarch and this prompted the conspiracy against him.

Plot

The story line covers the intrigue against Caesar, the most famous name in ancient Roman history, his consequent assassination, and the civil war that followed.

Themes

The following are the major themes in the play. You may want to consider others:

Conflict

The play can be seen as a study of conflicts, between groups, between individuals, and within a person. The play begins with a situation of conflict when the tribunes confront the common people; there is open conflict when Caesar is struck down; the opposing forces clash towards the end of the play; there is conflict among the triumvirate; Brutus quarrels with Cassius at Sardis; Brutus experiences conflict in his mind when he debates with himself over the killing of Caesar.

Rhetoric and Persuasion

The play explores the influence of rhetoric and persuasion. When a character succeeds in swaying his or her listener or listeners, Shakespeare makes it clear that it is a deliberate effort. Consider how: Cassius persuades Brutus to join in the conspiracy against Caesar; Portia persuades Brutus to reveal his secret to her; Calphurnia persuades Caesar who is in turn persuaded by Decius. Perhaps most memorable is Antony's rhetorical power in first persuading the conspirators of his sincerity and then the common people of the conspirators' treachery.

Honour and Duty

It deals with honour and duty: Brutus' whole involvement in the conspiracy hinges on this; Antony sees it as his honourable duty to avenge Caesar's death; Brutus and Cassius see it more honourable to die than be taken as prisoners and they are helped in this by their soldiers who see it as their duty. There are enough references to honour in the course of the play to establish its importance as a theme.

Power and Ambition

The play explores power and political ambition. It shows the lengths that individuals will go to achieve dominance over people, from Caesar to Cassius, to Antony, to Octavius. It is Caesar's ambition to have absolute control that triggers the conspiracy; Cassius' envy of Caesar and his own frustrated ambition cause him to instigate Brutus into joining the conspiracy; Antony's and Octavius' separate ambitions prevent them from agreeing on several occasions.

Friendship and Love

It examines friendship and love: the relationship between Brutus and Cassius is looked at closely; Brutus' feelings for his good friend Caesar are put to the test; we look at the love Brutus has for Portia; we see the loyalty of friends who remain to the end.

Omens and Fate

The play also looks into the role of supernatural signs and man's unavoidable destiny. The omens and the supernatural happenings seem to suggest that they play a part in prophesying death. All the main characters, as well as some minor ones, make some reference to death. Caesar, Cinna, Brutus and Cassius speak of the signs before they die.

THE PLAY

Act I, scene i

It is February the 15th, the feast of the Lupercal. The tribunes, Marullus and Flavius, meet a group of common people whom they reprimand for not being in their work clothes. They learn from a cobbler that the group has taken a holiday to celebrate Caesar's victory over Pompey's sons, and to watch his triumphant procession. Angered, Marullus reminds them that not too long ago, they had been supporters of Pompey, and rebukes them for being fickle in their political loyalties. Flavius tells them to weep tears of repentance for this show of disloyalty. Guiltily, the crowd leaves. Marullus and Flavius decide to remove all the decorations from Caesar's statues and disperse any gathering of people they come across in the street.

Comment

This is an arresting opening to the play. A lively encounter between the authorities and the common people sets the mood for the rest of the play, and prepares the audience for further conflicts. The audience's attention is brought immediately to the man in the centre of the conflicts, Caesar, who is popular with the crowd but hated by the tribunes. This hostility is clearly conveyed in Marullus' emotional speech of rebuke to the group. He shames them by pointing out that they have no reason to rejoice [lines 31-54], because Caesar has not defeated a foreigner, but a fellow Roman, whom they once had loved and supported. His speech succeeds in making the people feel guilty. Ashamed, they move silently away. At the end of the scene, in an act of open defiance, Flavius instructs Marullus to pluck the 'growing feathers' from 'Caesar's wings'. This scene shows the fickleness of the common people and how easily they are persuaded to shift from a celebratory mood to one of penitence. This trait of theirs is further explored in the play and proves to be important in contributing to the conspirators' downfall. It is also clear, in this scene, that there is opposition to Caesar, despite the public celebration.

Act I, scene ii

Caesar makes a grand entrance. He instructs Calphurnia to stand in Antony's path as he runs, so as to cure her of her barrenness. A soothsayer warns him to beware the Ides of March, but Caesar brushes him aside, and orders the procession to move on. Cassius, left alone with Brutus, starts working on him. He tells Brutus that he has important matters to discuss with him. On hearing a shout, Brutus comments that he fears that Caesar is being offered a crown. Cassius takes this as his cue to start his tirade against Caesar. He highlights two occasions when Caesar showed himself to be weak: once, Cassius had to save him from drowning; another time, Caesar suffered from fever in Spain. He points out that they have allowed themselves to be oppressed under Caesar's power and reminds Brutus that it was his ancestor who drove out the last king of Rome. Brutus tells Cassius that he will think about what he has said and assures him that he will not stand by and allow Rome to suffer oppression. Caesar and his party return, and Caesar on seeing Cassius, warns Antony to be wary of thin, deep-thinking men [lines 192-195]. From Casca, Brutus and Cassius learn that Antony had offered Caesar a crown three times which Caesar had refused, to the cheers of the crowd. He also reports that Caesar had suffered an epileptic fit and that Marullus and Flavius have been stripped of their positions for removing the decorations from Caesar's statues. When Cassius is left alone, he reveals that he intends to write anonymous letters and throw them into Brutus' house to ensure that Brutus joins in the conspiracy.

Comment

At this early point of the play, attention is focused on the titular character, Julius Caesar. Shakespeare reveals an undertow of discontent among the patricians at Caesar's growing power. This is Caesar's first appearance and immediately, he strikes us as a figure who commands respect and fear. When he speaks, everyone is silent. His instructions are carried out without question. Further, he shows himself to be a shrewd judge of character when he accurately sums up Cassius' character [lines 201-210]. His arrogance is seen in the way he insists that he is incapable of feeling fear. Caesar is a consummate politician who is constantly in the public eye, and he makes a point of maintaining his popularity with the people. This he achieves when he refuses the crown and when he offers his life to them. This scene also shows the contrasting natures of Brutus and Cassius. Brutus is mainly calm and restrained, while Cassius, consumed with passion, is unable to control his feelings of envy and hatred toward Caesar. Cassius knows Brutus' character very well and he shows this in his skilful persuasion of Brutus. He uses flattery on him; he appeals to his sense of honour and to his patriotism; he makes it appear his moral duty to join in the conspiracy [lines 159-162].

Cassius himself is motivated by more personal reasons of jealousy and hatred. The note of contempt towards Caesar is unmistakable when he describes him as '[a] man of such a feeble temper'. Cassius reveals that he is capable of resorting to unscrupulous means to ensure that Brutus is won over to the conspiracy. Casca defers to Caesar in public, but he is blunt and sarcastic when giving the report of the proceedings. Clearly, he despises Caesar, but does not allow this to show in public. However, it does not escape Cassius, and he wins him over in the next scene, with little difficulty.

Act I, scene iii

Casca cowers in fear at the terrifying storm. He tells Cicero of the strange signs he has seen: fire dropping from the sky; a slave whose burning hand left him unharmed, a lion which went by him without attacking, a hundred women, pale at the sight of men on fire, walking up and down the street and the owl hooting and shrieking at mid-day. Casca takes these strange phenomena as a warning from the gods. Cicero, on the other hand, seems unperturbed. When Cassius enters, he tells Casca that he has been tempting the lightning to strike him. He suggests that the strange happenings are a sign that the gods are displeased that Caesar has grown too powerful. When he learns that Caesar will be offered the kingship of the Roman territories outside Italy, Cassius declares that he is ready to kill himself to remain free. He says that Caesar has become a tyrant only because Romans have become weak. He then challenges Casca to betray him if he were a willing slave of Caesar's. Casca assures Cassius that he is ready to join him in any enterprise to put things right in Rome. At this, Cassius reveals that he has already got together a group of noble Romans who will meet him later that night at Pompey's porch. Before he leaves, he tells Cinna to place anonymous letters in various places in Brutus' house.

Comment

The storm, with its strange omens, is a Shakespearean device to suggest the impending social disorder. The intrigue is brewing as Cassius gathers support among the eminent men of Rome. It reaches a climax in the assassination of Caesar, but this in turn signals the start of social chaos in Rome which is not resolved until the conspirators are defeated.

The storm affects the characters differently. Cinna and Casca are terrified by the strange signs. Cicero remains composed [line 14]. Cassius uses it to impress Casca with a show of manliness. He jumps at the opportunity to win Casca over and it proves to be an easier task than with Brutus. Without at first being too open about his feelings against Caesar, Cassius plays on Casca's fear of the supernatural. He offers his own interpretation of the meaning of the storm, vaunts his willingness to die, and shames him with a rebuke of all weak Romans [lines 82-83]. Cassius succeeds because he is able to adapt his method of persuasion to the character at hand. With Casca, he does not waste time in intellectual cajoling. Instead, he exploits Casca's fear and forces his hand with a challenge.

Act II, scene i

Alone in his garden, Brutus tries to resolve the conflict in his mind. He has decided that Caesar has to die, but he has no motive to strike him down, as Caesar has not, as yet, done anything that deserves death. Thus, Brutus reasons that once Caesar is crowned, as general tendencies go, he will be corrupt. To prevent this abuse of power, he must be killed. Lucius brings Brutus letters that Cinna had earlier placed in his garden. Brutus is moved by them and decides that he should rise to the occasion and save Rome from tyranny.

The conspirators arrive. When Cassius suggests they take an oath, Brutus declines saying that no oath is needed among honourable, trusted Romans armed with a just cause. Cassius then suggests including Cicero in the conspiracy. Brutus rejects the idea, saying that he will never be part of something that someone else has started. Brutus disagrees with Cassius a third time when the latter suggests killing Antony as he could become dangerous. Brutus is determined to keep Caesar's killing an act of sacrifice in order to purify Rome. To kill Antony as well would appear excessive. Besides, Brutus believes Antony is powerless without Caesar. The conspirators consider the likelihood of Caesar leaving his house that day, as his augurers might prevent him because of all the strange omens of the previous day. Decius assures them that he will persuade Caesar to go to the Capitol. Before they leave, they decide to include Caius Ligarius in the conspiracy.

Portia, who is troubled by the late night visit, pleads with Brutus to tell her what is causing him to behave strangely. He has lost his appetite, and has been restless and preoccupied for the last few days. She appeals to his love for her and their marriage vows, to be allowed to share his secrets. She reminds that she has proved her fortitude by patiently bearing a wound that she has given herself. Brutus is visibly moved and promises to tell her everything. Caius Ligarius arrives and promises to support Brutus in any noble enterprise he has in mind.

Comment

In his soliloquy, Brutus shows himself torn between his loyalty to his friend Caesar and his love for his country. Brutus must have been long aware of Caesar's growing power, but it is not until Cassius whets him against Caesar that he decides he must be killed. Having decided on the course of action to take against Caesar, Brutus' conscience troubles him. He is no murderer and has to have a motive, noble enough to justify something as drastic as the killing of a friend. At this point, he begins to rationalise. Judging by Caesar's present behaviour, there is no reason to kill him [lines 19-21]. Therefore, Brutus convinces himself that Caesar will accept the crown eventually, and once given absolute power, will abuse it and turn all Romans into slaves. In order to keep Rome a republic and free from Caesar's oppression, he concludes, 'it must be by his death'. He decides to kill Caesar, to uphold a principle that he absolutely believes in. Yet it has not been an easy decision. He has suffered sleeplessness and 'an insurrection' within his mind. However, the letters exhorting him to rise up against Caesar clinch this decision. Once he embarks on this course of action, he does not waver. He assumes command of the situation immediately, and the other conspirators give in to his suggestions without question. When he vetoes Cassius' suggestion that they take an oath, no one objects. In quick succession, Brutus turns down two more suggestions of Cassius. He refuses to include Cicero in the conspiracy and probably deprives himself of the wisdom of a respected senator. His decision not to kill Antony reflects two different aspects of his character. First, it is not envy or anger but his duty to Rome that has prompted this line of action. Once he has removed the immediate source of danger to

Rome's liberty, he has no wish for further violence [lines 166-177]. Next, Brutus shows himself naive and lacking in political acumen in the way he underestimates Antony and fails to safeguard his position.

This is the only scene where we see Brutus in his role as a husband. The courtesy and graciousness that he extends to his wife and the warm affection that he obviously feels for her add a human dimension to his character.

This scene is also the first of Portia's two appearances in the play. Here, she is a strong and courageous wife whose sole concern is with her husband's welfare. Her next appearance however, reveals another side of her.

Act II, scene ii

The storm continues. Caesar tells his servant to bid the priests to offer sacrifices and read the results. Calphurnia, frightened by the strange omens, begs Caesar not to leave the house. Caesar dismisses her fears saying that the signs pertain to the world, not to him alone. When the servant returns with an unfavourable divination, Caesar interprets this as a challenge for him to go to the Senate House. However, Calphurnia, who has had a terrifying dream about Caesar, goes on her knees to beg him to stay. Caesar finally gives in. When Decius arrives to take him to the Senate House, he tells him that he will not be attending the meeting. When Decius asks him for a reason, Caesar tells him that it is enough that the senators are told that it is his will. When pressed further, he reveals that Calphurnia dreamt that his statue spouted blood while many smiling Romans washed their hands in it. Decius offers his own flattering interpretation: the dream signifies that Caesar will give new blood to Rome. He also lures Caesar with the news that the senators have decided to offer him a crown that day but may change their minds if he does not turn up. Furthermore, Caesar will be the object of their ridicule for being influenced by his wife's dreams. Caesar is persuaded and decides to attend the meeting.

Comment

This domestic scene between Caesar and Calphurnia parallels the earlier scene between Brutus and Portia. However, it lacks the warmth and intimacy of the earlier scene, at least on Caesar's part. We see the private Caesar who is as proud of his fearlessness at home as the public Caesar is in front of a crowd [lines10-12; 32-33]. He likens himself to 'Danger's more dangerous twin brother and shows a haughty disregard for the senators. Although he gives in to Calphurnia's pleadings, he changes his mind when lured by the prospect of being crowned. His susceptibility to flattery enables Decius to succeed in his persuasion. The scene increases in suspense as Caesar graciously welcomes his would-be murderers. At its close, Caesar says to Brutus, 'And we, like friends, will straightway go together'. The irony of this remark prepares us for greater tension, especially between Caesar and Brutus, as the characters head for the scene of the assassination.

Act II, scene iii

Artemidorus reads a schedule listing the conspirators by name. He intends to warn Caesar with it as he passes by, on his way to the Capital.

Comment

This short scene is intended to heighten the anticipation. We wonder if Artemidorus will reach Caesar in time to warn him. Again, the audience is made aware that there are admirers of Caesar like Artemidorus, who will risk being at the site of the planned murder in order to try and save him. Despite the unflattering portrayal of Caesar up to this point, we are gripped with apprehension for the deed that is about to take place.

Act II, scene iv

Portia, having been told of the conspiracy, waits nervously outside her house. She tells Lucius to go and observe what is happening at the Senate House. She longs to unburden herself of the secret she is carrying and finds it difficult to be quiet. Before Lucius leaves, they meet a soothsayer who is trying to warn Caesar of the danger that he is in. Finally, Lucius goes off and Portia is left in a state of anxiety.

Comment

In this scene, Portia who earlier showed her husband proof of her strength, finds herself under a tremendous strain. The manly courage that she claims to have is missing as she complains 'how weak a woman's heart is'. The incoherent instructions she gives Lucius reflect her state of anxiety. Indeed, her present emotional and psychological state foreshadows the moment of her death, after she falls 'distract' and swallows fire during Brutus' absence. At this point, another minor character, the soothsayer, appears, adding to the dramatic tension. Like Artemidorus, earlier, he is trying to warn Caesar. The characters' references to time make the audience conscious of how close the fateful moment is.

Act III scene i

The soothsayer and Artemidorus try to warn Caesar as he goes up to the Senate house. Popilius Lena's remark triggers off a panicky reaction from a nervous Cassius and he is ready to commit suicide. Brutus tells him to keep calm and points out that Caesar remains smiling. The conspirators behave according to their plan. Metellus begins to plead before Caesar who interrupts him

with a haughty rejection of his petition. He is not about to bend the law to recall Metellus's brother, who has been justly banished. Brutus, Cassius, Cinna and Decius, in turn, grovel in front of Caesar, who spurns them all. Casca takes his cue and stabs him, followed by the rest of the conspirators. When Caesar sees Brutus stabbing him, he stops resisting and dies. Pandemonium follows and Brutus tries to pacify the people while he instructs the conspirators to dip their hands in Caesar's blood and cry out 'Peace, freedom and liberty'.
A servant of Antony arrives asking for safe passage for his master, who wishes to meet with the conspirators to discover why Caesar was killed. Brutus guarantees to give him an answer that will satisfy him and promises that he will be unharmed.

When Antony arrives he immediately mourns over the body of Caesar, ignoring the conspirators. He offers his life to them, but Brutus assures him that they do not intend to harm him but welcome him as a friend. Cassius offers him a position in their new government while Brutus again assures him that he will be given reasons for Caesar's death. Antony shakes the hands of the conspirators one by one, but on looking at the body of Caesar starts grieving over him again. This worries Cassius and he asks him to clarify his position with them. Antony assures him that he is a friend and hopes that they will soon be able to show him cause for their actions. He also asks for permission to speak at Caesar's funeral. Brutus complies immediately but Cassius warns him that Antony will rouse the people. Brutus confidently assures him he will speak from the pulpit first and will set conditions that Antony has to keep to, namely: he must not blame them but may praise Caesar; he must tell the people he speaks with the permission of the conspirators.

When Antony is left alone, he bursts out in a passionate speech of anguish and rage, swearing vengeance. He predicts that death and civil war will be the order of the day. A messenger comes to inform him that Octavius is on his way to Rome. Antony tells the messenger to observe what happens at the funeral and take the news back to his master.

Comment

There is much bustling at the beginning of the scene and this adds to the mounting tension before the assassination. The soothsayer, then Artemidorus, then Decius, then Artemidorus again, all clamour for Caesar's attention. Cassius is excitable [lines 19-22], while Brutus is characteristically unruffled [lines 22-24]. Caesar is seen at the peak of his arrogance and with his arrogant remarks elevates himself almost to the level of the gods. At this point of the play, Caesar loses much of our sympathy and we perhaps momentarily wish the conspirators would carry on with their task. However, the killing itself is brutal. Caesar's last remark before he gives up is touching: 'Et tu, Brute?' It conveys such a profound sense of betrayal that the audience may wish for the clocks to turn back. Equally horrifying is the way the conspirators smear their hands with Caesar's blood. This brings to mind Calphurnia's ominous dream. Brutus has finally performed his great sacrifice but it is neither holy nor solemn. Instead, the people flee in panic and in the midst of the chaos Brutus realises he has to restore order.

Even before normality returns, Antony sends his servant to test the situation. He has no real intention of joining the conspirators who have just brutally murdered his leader. It is all part of a clever strategy to ensure that he remain unharmed and to give the conspirators a feeling of security. While he is certainly unsettled by the incident, he quickly gains control of the situation. His laments over Caesar's bloody corpse do not contain an indictment of the killers. His flattery of the conspirators when he offers his life to the 'choice and master spirits of this age' puts them in an awkward position. Brutus is defensive and assures Antony that they do not intend to harm him and welcomes him as a friend. When Antony shakes the hands of the conspirators in a gesture of reconciliation, it is mere politicking. It certainly fools Brutus who allows him to speak at the funeral.

Brutus intends to show the people that he bears no malice and that he did care for Caesar by according him a proper funeral, including a close friend's eulogy. In his passionate outburst after the conspirators leave, Antony reveals his true feelings. His rage and anguish are intense, his desire for revenge, blood-thirsty, inspired by love for the ruin of 'the noblest man/That ever lived in the tide of times'. The scene ends on a note of anticipation of the funeral scene.

Act III, scene ii

Brutus and Cassius separately speak to the people. Brutus addresses an angry crowd demanding an explanation for Caesar's murder. He appeals to them to use their reason to judge what he, as an honourable man, has to say. As Caesar's friend, he loved him as much as anyone there, but his greater love for Rome made it necessary for him to kill Caesar. Had he been allowed to live, Caesar would have made them all slaves. Thus, he received what he deserved, 'death for his ambition'. The only people who would, therefore, object to the killing would be those willing to be slaves. Naturally, no one objects. He ensures the people that the reasons for the killing have been recorded and kept in the Capitol. As Antony arrives with the body of Caesar, Brutus offers his life to the people, who want him to be Caesar instead. He entreats the crowd to remain and listen to Antony's speech. Antony begins by disclaiming that he has come to praise Caesar. He says he speaks with Brutus' permission but proceeds to invalidate Brutus' claim that Caesar was ambitious. Caesar gave ransom money to the state treasury; he cried when the poor suffered during a famine; he refused the crown three times. Do these actions speak of ambition? He then criticises them for not mourning him, a man they all once loved. He pauses, apparently overcome with grief, and the people react with sympathy, He goes on to plant the idea of mutiny before he mentions the will. However, he withholds the will itself and tells the people that he will be doing the honourable men who have killed Caesar wrong by revealing it. The people are enraged and call the conspirators 'traitors'. Antony comes down and shows them the mantle-covered body of Caesar instead. Deliberating on the holes in the mantle, he identifies those made by Brutus, Cassius and Casca, specifically. When he sees them moved, he reveals the body. The people are horrified. Antony tells them that he is an unskilled speaker. However, if he were Brutus, he would be able to stir their spirits and make them rise up in mutiny. On hearing this, the people are ready to revolt. However, Antony holds them back to read them the will which leaves them seventy-five drachmas each, and Caesar's garden, summer houses and orchards. The people's rage reaches fever pitch. In a mood bent on violence and destruction, they rush away to burn and kill.

A messenger comes announcing that Octavius has arrived, and that Brutus and Cassius have already fled Rome.

Comment

The central interest in this scene is the speeches of Brutus and Antony. These reveal a contrast between the two speakers' understanding of human nature and their effectiveness as politicians. Brutus' immediate task is to pacify a crowd angered and bewildered by the killing of Caesar. He is confident that his cause will make itself clear and vindicate the assassination. This is his crucial task—to convince the people that Caesar was ambitious for absolute power and would have taken away their birthright and made them slaves. He, thus, needs to awaken them to the very principle that prompted his own part in the killing.

His speech itself is well-prepared and eloquent, though his disdain for the commoners is apparent even from the start. He tells them to 'be silent that [they] may hear' and to 'awake [their] senses.' Employing artful oratory, he calms the crowd by proclaiming his love for Caesar and the reason he had to die. His use of rhetorical questions overwhelms the crowd: 'Had you rather Caesar were living, and die all slaves, than that Caesar were dead to live all free men?' It points out the dire consequences that will befall the commoners if Caesar had become king and is intended to move them to accept Caesar's murder. At the end of Brutus' speech, the people show him tremendous support, despite not fully understanding what Brutus claims to have attained for them. When Antony takes the pulpit, Brutus' fragile hold over the people is broken.

There are several reasons for Brutus' failure. One is his total ignorance of the nature of his audience. As a stoic, who makes it a practice to keep his feelings in check, he fails to realise he is dealing with a group, largely capable of reacting only with their emotions. He also makes the mistake of treating the common people as his intellectual equal, using abstract, albeit beautifully phrased arguments [lines 21-29]. However, these, without concrete illustrations, remain quite out of the depth of his listeners. At the onset of his speech, Brutus tells the crowd to 'be patient till the last', and 'be silent, that [they] may hear'. He talks down to his audience and in doing so fails to make a connection with them. His tone remains unchanged for the rest of his speech. He maintains aloofness and speaks with an aura of authority that silences his audience. Brutus' final mistake is to leave Antony alone with the people. In an alarming display of naiveté, he pushes caution aside, and provides Antony with the opportunity he wants. The crowd's reaction to Brutus' speech reveals how little they have absorbed it. They want to make him another Caesar, when all along he has been trying to tell them there is no place for one in republican Rome.

When Antony takes the pulpit, he faces a hostile group of people, who have just made Brutus their new hero. However, he comes better equipped than Brutus. Together with his understanding of the common people, he has a bagful of persuasive tools and a most effective prop, Caesar's body.

His first words dispel any suspicion that he has come to make a lengthy eulogy on Caesar. His tone is tentative, questioning, puzzled. The people probably see this as a reflection of their own uncertainties. Antony places on one side his own experiences of Caesar's virtues against what the 'honourable men' call his ambition. Illustrating his speech with incidents that the people are familiar with, such as Caesar filling the 'general coffer' with ransom money, Caesar weeping in times of famine, and Caesar refusing the crown, Antony shows Caesar to be sensitive and generous. His elaborate proof of Caesar's lack of ambition contradicts Brutus' earlier charge. Unlike Brutus, Antony boldly ranges through a gamut of emotions to capture the attention of his audience. Gaining confidence after he destroys Brutus' accusation, he scolds the people for their hard-heartedness towards Caesar whom they once loved. To test how far he has succeeded with the crowd, he pauses, overcome with grief, and is encouraged by their show of sympathy.

Antony laments Caesar's sudden fall from glory, and before introducing the will, he takes a parting shot at the 'honourable men'. The term 'honourable' which he uses a total of ten times, has by this time become suspect. He teases the people with the will, which he does 'not mean to read', but reveals enough to whet their greed and enrage the 'heirs' of Caesar so that they call Brutus and the other conspirators 'traitors, villains, murderers'. At this point, Antony employs a carefully timed ploy to ensure the fickle crowd is completely swayed.

He comes down from the pulpit to reveal Caesar's bloody mantle. Antony deliberates on each and every hole in it as he condemns each of the ringleaders of the conspiracy, by name. He establishes a feeling of unity with the people by speaking of Caesar's death as a nation's tragedy. While his listeners are at the height of their grief and guilt, he shows them Caesar's bloody corpse. It puts them in a frenzy. They cry for revenge as they swear their allegiance to Antony. But he is not finished with them. Suggesting that Brutus had skilfully deceived his listeners earlier [lines 210-211], he tells them that he speaks merely from the heart. Had he Brutus' skill, he would make them rise up in mutiny, [lines 219-223] thus, suggesting the action they should take. Antony delivers his final stroke by reading them the will. After this, there is no stopping them.

Act III, scene iii

Cinna, the poet, has had a dream where he was dining with Caesar. The mob comes across him on the street and kills him for his bad verses.

Comment

This short scene captures the violence that Antony's speech has incited and prepares the audience for further conflicts. The mindless killing of Cinna reflects a grimmer development of the malleable character of the common people, seen in Act I, who have now become a mob. Cinna's portentous dream underlines the important role of omens in the play.

Act IV, scene i

The triumvirate, Antony, Octavius and Lepidus, are marking the names of their enemies for execution. This includes Lepidus' brother and Antony's nephew. Antony sends Lepidus off to bring him Caesar's will so that he can cut off part of the people's legacy. In Lepidus' absence, Antony reveals to Octavius that he thinks Lepidus is unworthy of sharing power with them, and should be treated as a beast of burden to carry out their dirty work and then stripped of his power when he is no longer useful. Octavius comments that he is a good soldier, but Antony likens him to his horse which has to be given directions to perform its task. Lepidus should therefore be treated as a mere tool to be exploited. Antony then reveals that Brutus and Cassius are consolidating their armies and he and Octavius must prepare to join forces to meet this threat.

Comment

The triumvirate shows a disturbing hardheartedness in the way they check off names for execution. Lepidus and Antony trade relatives in a business-like manner [lines 2-6].There is a sense of recklessness here, which is in marked contrast to Brutus' determination not to harm anyone else besides Caesar. Antony is seen here at one of his worst moments. His exploitation of Lepidus, a 'tried and valiant soldier' shows callousness. Also, Antony dishonestly contrives to cut off part of the people's legacy left by Caesar. Earlier, he had used the will as bait to turn the people against the conspirators. There is an undercurrent of opposition in Octavius' appreciation of Lepidus. His independence of thought is again seen later on the battlefield. Antony's reminder to Octavius of his greater experience suggests his need to exert control over him.

Act IV, scene ii

The exiled armies of Brutus and Cassius are joining forces at Sardis. Brutus complains to Pindarus, Cassius' slave, that he is annoyed at something Cassius has done. Lucilius comments on his less than warm reception at Cassius' camp. The two generals meet and their first words to each other are heated exchanges. They decide to continue their discussion more privately, away from their soldiers.

Comment

Brutus and Cassius appear to be feeling the strain of exile. It has already taken a toll on their relationship. The quarrel intensifies in the following scene as the two become further estranged.

Act IV, scene iii

Brutus and Cassius continue their quarrel in their tents. Cassius accuses Brutus of punishing his friend for taking bribes despite his personal intervention. He tells Brutus that it is not the time to be over scrupulous. Brutus makes a counter charge of Cassius' own dishonesty, and reminds him that they killed Caesar in the name of justice and asks if they are going to taint the deed with corruption. Cassius rejoins by saying that he is a more experienced soldier and knows what to do under the circumstances. Brutus reacts in scorn and tells him that he will in future merely condescend to laugh at him when he shows his temper. He then challenges Cassius' claim that he is an abler soldier and reveals another reason for his anger. Brutus has requested a sum of money to pay his soldiers from Cassius but has been turned down. Cassius denies this but says that Brutus should be more tolerant of his faults. Then giving in to despair, he calls on the enemies to avenge themselves on him alone, and offers his life to Brutus. At this, Brutus' anger is dispelled. He tells Cassius to keep his sword and be angry whenever he wants.

As the generals are making up, a poet forces his way in to try and reconcile them. He is unceremoniously removed. Brutus then reveals what has added to his strain. He has learnt that Portia has killed herself in his absence, by swallowing coals. Cassius is overcome with grief. As they drink wine to forget their quarrel, Messala arrives with news that Antony and Octavius are approaching Philippi with their troops. They also learn from him that one hundred senators, including Cicero, have been killed. Finally, Messala reluctantly tells Brutus that Portia is dead. Brutus takes the news calmly and quickly goes on to matters at hand. He suggests marching to Philippi but Cassius thinks it is better to wait at Sardis so that the enemies tire themselves out by marching to them. Brutus overrules his suggestion by pointing out that by cutting the enemy off at Philippi, they will be prevented from strengthening themselves with recruits from the villages. Besides, their own armies are as strong as they will ever be, so this is the most opportune time to meet the enemy. Cassius gives in and the two part in a mood of renewed friendship. Alone, Brutus gets ready to read. But he sees the ghost of Caesar which tells him that he will see him again at Philippi, and then vanishes. Brutus prepares for the march.

Comment

The quarrel reveals a facet of the characters of Brutus and Cassius that we have not seen before. Under the tremendous strain of the exile and news of his wife's death, Brutus loses control of his feelings. He uncharacteristically gives vent to a temper tantrum, most uncharacteristic of a stoic. He is verbally abusive to Cassius, even resorting to name-calling in the quarrel [lines 37 and 40]. Cassius, on the other hand, comes across not as the excitable hot-head of the earlier scenes, but as a vulnerable, tolerant friend who puts up with Brutus' harangue. Cassius is unable, or unwilling, to muster enough anger to retaliate with the same vehemence. In this quarrel, our sympathy tends to lie with Cassius as he bears the brunt of Brutus' temper outburst. Furthermore, it is he who first makes the attempt to end the quarrel, as he offers his life to Brutus [lines 93-105]. Cassius too appears to be more tolerant than Brutus towards the meddlesome poet [line 135].

It is in this scene that Brutus is seen at the height of his self-righteousness [lines 66-69]. Brutus accuses Cassius of having an 'itching-palm' and declares that he could never stoop to 'raise money by evil means', yet he stretches out his hand to Cassius for the same 'vile trash' to pay his troops.

Later in the scene, Brutus makes a costly mistake in planning the battle strategy. Again Cassius gives in against his better judgement, unwilling to engage n another argument. In a quieter mood, at the end of the scene, Brutus' words to Lucius, Varo and Claudius reflect the extreme kindness to his underlings that is characteristic of him. It is significant that the ghost appears here. This Shakespearian device contributes a greater sense of Brutus' impending doom. Brutus sees it a second time at Phillipi and he knows that his 'hour is come'.

Act V, scene i

Octavius comments that Brutus and Cassius have, against expectations, decided to attack them at Philippi, However, Antony believes that this is only to give a false impression of their courage.

He tells Octavius to keep to the left side of the field but the latter decides to disobey him and occupy the right side. They meet Brutus and Cassius for a parley. During the exchanges, Antony reminds them that their battle is still over Caesar's death. Antony and Octavius consider themselves the avengers of Caesar, and Brutus is still convinced of the justice of his action. There are further taunts before Octavius challenges them to come to the field.

Cassius reveals to Messala how he has grown superstitious and has begun to believe in signs which he takes as premonitions of impending doom. Cassius and Brutus talk about what they will do if they lose the battle. Because of his philosophy, Brutus sees suicide as a cowardly act and blames Cato for killing himself. But he tells Cassius that he will never allow himself to be humiliated and led in chains. Both express the feeling that whatever happens, that day will end their great work which began on the Ides of March.

Comment

Octavius's strong personality, hinted at earlier, is further revealed in this scene. Though younger and a less experienced soldier, he does very much as he pleases, not just in deference to Antony's will [lines 18 and 20]. Together with Antony, he takes on the role of Caesar's avengers and is equally vocal in exchanging insults with Brutus and Cassius. He exudes confidence and appears even more eager than Antony to test the conspirators' skills on the battle field.

The face-to-face encounter with Brutus and Cassius ignites Antony's rage and this is reflected in the invectives he hurls at them: 'apes', 'hounds', 'bondmen', 'cur'. During the parley, Brutus and Cassius answer their enemies' verbal attacks blow by blow. On their own, however, their speeches sound very pessimistic. Curiously, both express feelings that are contrary to their respective philosophies. Cassius, an epicurean, has begun to become superstitious and to see significance in the appearance of 'ravens, crows and kites' in place of the eagles. Brutus, a stoic, declares that although he is against suicide, he will never allow himself to be led in chains, as Antony's prisoner. There is a touching note of resignation and finality in their 'everlasting farewell' [lines 115-124] and indeed, this is the last time they see each other.

Act V, scene ii

Brutus gives the order to attack Octavius's troops as he senses a lack of enthusiasm in that wing.

Comment

Brutus commits his final strategic error when he gives the signal for his men to attack.

Act V, scene iii

Cassius' men have retreated as Antony's forces attack. Cassius has had to kill his own soldiers to stop them from fleeing. It appears that Brutus has attacked too early and his men have been wasting time plundering the camps, while Cassius' own camp is surrounded by Antony's men. He takes to the hills as he sees his camp on fire. Sending Titinius down to survey the approaching troops, he tells Pindarus to observe from the hills as he is short-sighted. Pindarus reports that Titinius has been surrounded and captured by the enemies who shout in jubilation. Cassius despairs as he helplessly watches his friend's capture. Promising Pindarus his freedom, he instructs him to hold his sword while he runs on it. Pindarus performs this final duty for Cassius and then runs away.

Titinius and Messala return with news that Brutus has overthrown Octavius' troops and a wreath of victory for Cassius, only to find him dead. While Messala leaves to tell Brutus the sad news, Titinius kills himself in an act of loyalty.

Comment

Cassius meets his death in circumstances that are not entirely unexpected. All along, he has shown himself to be ruled by passion and impulse. Ready to give up his life when things threaten to go wrong, Cassius yields to despair a little too early. His readiness to accept Pindarus' words reflects his defeatist attitude and his general pessimism With his last breath, he calls on Caesar as he turns the very sword that killed Caesar on himself [lines 45-46]. It is significant too, that Brutus attributes Cassius' and Titinius' deaths to Caesar's spirit [lines 94-96]. Although Cassius has had to turn on his own men to prevent them from running away, he has inspired great loyalty in some of them. Pindarus remains with him till the end. Titinius speaks of Cassius in admiring terms and even kills himself for love of him.

Act V, scene iv

The fighting continues. Cato, Brutus' brother-In-law, meets his death in a heroic way. Lucilius pretends to be Brutus and is captured. When he is brought to Antony, he tells him that Brutus will never be taken alive. Antony treats him with courtesy and continues the search for Brutus.

Comment

The bravery of Brutus' men contrasts with the uneven conduct of Cassius' men. Cato dies in action; Lucilius offers himself to be killed in order to protect Brutus. His faith in his general is summed. up when he says '...no man shall ever take alive the noble Brutus'. Antony recognizes a brave soldier when he sees one and immediately decides to take him into his service.

Act V, scene v

Brutus, with the last of his men, is resting on a rock. He approaches them, one by one, to ask them to help him kill himself. Horrified and saddened by the request, they refuse. Brutus remarks that his end is near and it is more noble to end it all himself than to wait for the enemy to do it for him. The enemy troops are fast approaching and before he bids them all goodbye, he expresses his appreciation that all his men have been loyal to him. He remarks that he will gain more glory than Antony and Octavius, by losing the battle that lay, as he has fought for justice. Before the enemies march in, Strato holds the sword while Brutus runs on it.

Octavius promises to take Brutus' men into his service. On seeing Brutus' body, Antony pays a brief, but moving tribute to Brutus, Arrangements are made for Brutus' body t lie in state in Octavius' camp while they celebrate their victory.

Comment

Brutus' men remain loyal to him right to the end. Dardanius, Clitus and Volumnius cannot bring themselves to help Brutus kill himself. Strato gives in to Brutus only after he pleads with him at the last moment. When Strato is found by Antony and Octavius, he boldly announces that 'Brutus only overcame himself'.

Just as Cassius calls on Caesar just before he dies, Brutus dies with Caesar's name on his lips. It seems that Caesar's spirit has hounded them right to their graves. Antony's tribute to Brutus sums up the general feeling towards him. Despite leading the murderous conspiracy, his motives and character, summed up in Antony's words [lines 68-75] are far nobler than those of the other conspirators.

CHARACTERS

The characters in the play reveal themselves in their speeches and in what others say of them. How we see these characters is influenced by our interpretation of their speeches. There is really no single acceptable way of looking at characters, especially characters as complex as those in 'Julius Caesar'. However, we must make sure that our own understanding of the characters in the play is based on textual evidence.

Julius Caesar

While both major and minor characters are introduced in the first three acts, it is Julius Caesar's physical presence which dominates each scene that he appears in. He fills the thoughts of men, and events are focused on him, reaching a climax in his assassination in Act III. Although he dies midway in the play, his influence continues to be felt in the last two acts.

How do we sum up Caesar's character? Caesar engages in no soul-baring soliloquies; he dies mid-way in the play; there are areas of ambivalence in his character. Yet he is compelling enough as a character for us to form an impression even at his first appearance. After the build-up in Act I, scene i, we anticipate an awe-inspiring figure, capable of arousing both adulation and resentment among the people. We are not disappointed as Caesar sweeps on stage, authoritative and dignified. We are struck by the way the other characters defer to him [Act I, scene ii, lines 2; 4; 5; 9-10; 14; 19].However, it is really his pride that stands out, above everything else we might have noticed about him. Both in public and in private, Caesar's arrogance is unmistakable. He tells Antony to beware of Cassius as he himself is incapable of fear nor is he ever likely to suffer this disease of lesser mortals: '... for always I am Caesar.' Later on, with Calphurnia, he compares himself to danger's 'elder and more terrible' brother'. This sense of self-importance reaches its peak just before he is killed when he elevates himself to the height of Olympus.

Equally clear is Caesar's courage. He is not afraid of death [Act II, scene ii, lines 32-37]. This is not just a vain boast. He shows courage in his fearless disregard of omens and the soothsayer's warnings and in the way he willingly dies when he sees Brutus stabbing him.

Caesar is a consummate politician and a crowd pleaser, who is capable of giving theatrical performances in public, as when his offers his throat to the people on the feast of the Lupercal. He is also a shrewd judge of character and is perceptive enough to see through Cassius, whose character is so brilliantly summed up in his speech to Antony [Act I, scene ii, lines 201-210]. Ironically, this talent of Caesar's does not prevent him from walking right into the conspirators' trap.

Because of areas of ambivalence in his character, Caesar remains a bit of an enigma. His attitude to signs and omens is inconsistent. Decius remarks that he has grown superstitious lately. When we first see him, he subjects Calphurnia to the superstitious practice of standing in the runner's way to cure her barrenness. Yet within minutes, he brushes aside the soothsayer. Later, he refuses to allow the strange omens of the evening keep him at home. He sends for the augurers, yet refuses to believe their divination.

Was Caesar ambitious? The tribunes believe so. So does Cassius. However, Cassius' views must be taken with some caution because he is obviously envious of Caesar. Brutus, in his soliloquy, says that he has not known him to be unreasonable or cruel but assumes that, 'He would be crowned'. Casca suggests that Caesar wanted the crown 'as he was very loath to lay his fingers off it'. However, Antony tells the people that he was not. Decius is able to persuade Caesar to go to the Capitol with the lure of the crown. Perhaps Caesar's eagerness to go, after Decius' revelation, gives us a better idea of his ambition than anything else.

In his personal relationships, Caesar shows courtesy and graciousness to his friends. Brutus and the rest are warmly treated before they leave for the senate. Brutus, notwithstanding the part he is to play in the killing, feels a deep regret even as he walks to the scene of the assassination. Antony's love for Caesar makes him take on the role of Caesar's avenger. His relentless pursuit of vengeance ends only with the death of Brutus. Such is the loyalty that Caesar has inspired in Antony. As a husband, Caesar is distant and cold. He humiliates his wife in public, admonishes her in Decius' presence and does not show her the respect and affection that Brutus has for Portia.

When Caesar dies, there is a general feeling of horror, because of the violent way he meets his death. However, it does not signal the end of Caesar's influence. Ironically, it is the spirit of Caesar, that Brutus wanted so badly to remove, that lives on. During Antony's soliloquy over his body, at the funeral scene, in the quarrel between the generals and during Brutus' and Cassius' last moments, Caesar's name echoes ominously. Caesar is still very much the point of reference, even in Act IV and Act V.

Brutus

If Caesar is something of an enigma, Brutus' character is no less complex. While Caesar is important as a force in the play, Brutus is surely the central character. The play traces his tragedy, from the time he shows himself troubled by Caesar's growing power in Act I, to his death in Act V. Moreover he is revealed to us as a character more than the others. Although we get glimpses into Cassius' and Antony's mind in their soliloquies, it is Brutus' inner self that we see wrestling to resolve a conflict in his soliloquies [Act II, scene i, lines10-34; 53-58; 61-69].

Shakespeare portrays Brutus as a basically highly principled man. There is no ambiguity about this. From the outset of the play, his honour is the one quality other characters stress and that is the reason he is needed to lead the conspiracy. Casca remarks that 'he sits high in all the people's hearts'; Cassius speaks about 'his worth and [their] great need of him'; the sick Caius Ligarius is ready to join any enterprise that 'the soul of Rome' leads. Brutus himself, in his somewhat self-conscious proclamation declares, 'Set honour in one eye and death in the other/And [he] will look on both indifferently.'

Brutus is an honourable man, not merely by reputation. Together with a deep sense of patriotism, made up of social consciousness and a sense of duty, his sincerity compels our admiration. In his soliloquy, we see Brutus' patriotism overriding his love for Caesar. In order to preserve his country's freedom, he is ready to sacrifice a friend. In Brutus' mind, it is essentially this – a sacrifice to be made for the general good. While this does not excuse him from the crime of assassination, it does clear him from any charge of personal gain. What is disturbing is the fact that Brutus makes his decision not on certain knowledge of Caesar's wrongdoings, 'since the quarrel/Will bear no colour for the thing he is,' but on his likely actions in the future. In this, Brutus may be accused of faulty reasoning, at best, or of being insincere, at worst. However, in order to kill him, Brutus needs to convince himself that Caesar will be a tyrannical king, and he comes to that decision with difficulty. Brutus' actions in sparing Antony and assuring the people that no one else will be hurt suggest that Brutus intends to uphold the sacrificial nature of the killing. His commitment to what he believes is a just cause is acknowledged even by Antony in his tribute to Brutus at the end of the play [Act V, scene v, lines 69-72].

While Brutus shows his resoluteness as a leader, he displays inadequacy in his lack of insight into the character of others. His own integrity is reflected in his decision not to take an oath during the conspirators meeting, but Brutus makes a simplistic assumption of other men's character. Earlier, he mistakenly sums up Casca as a 'blunt fellow' while Cassius is able to see deeper into his character. More importantly, Brutus fails to see the danger Antony poses to the conspirators. This example of political naiveté is intensified by his allowing Antony to speak alone to the people at Caesar's funeral. Similarly, Brutus' evaluation of the common people and his speech to them are based on his ignorance of how they think.

As a leader, Brutus has a tendency to consider his own opinions too highly. He is unable to take advice from others. His refusal to accept Cicero into the conspiracy shows how jealously he guards his position as a leader. Brutus is quick to reject all of Cassius' suggestions and as a result makes five grave errors in the play. Even after he has been proven wrong in his assessment of Antony, he insists on having his way in battle strategy, despite Cassius' greater experience as a soldier.

While Brutus' uprightness is maintained for most of the play, he is, at the same time, capable of being self-righteous and blind to his own faults. This reaches a height in the quarrel scene in the camp. Brutus is hard and unrelenting as he reprimands Cassius and condemns him for taking bribes. To counter Cassius' warning that his accusations may cause him to attack him, Brutus declares he is 'arm'd so strong in honesty,' that Cassius' threats ' pass by [him] as the idle wind.' He insists that he 'can raise no money by vile means', but he accuses Cassius of denying him the use of his ill-gotten money to pay his own troops [Act IV, scene iii, lines 69-70; 75-77]. Brutus' contradictory behaviour in this scene reflects the extreme stress he is under. The death of his wife, the difficulty of being in exile and the impending battle overwhelm Brutus, and his stoicism fails to restrain his emotions. Cassius comes across as more tolerant than Brutus in this scene.

Brutus' political role as leader of the conspiracy seems to bring out the worst in him; however, his conduct in his personal relationships reveals his nobler side. As a husband, Brutus' affection and respect towards his wife are displayed in the moving domestic scene in Act II, scene i. It is this closeness between husband and wife which makes the manner in which he accepts her death, remarkable. In three words, 'Portia is dead', Brutus succinctly sums up his grief and puts an end to Cassius' complaining. In dealing with this personal tragedy, Brutus shows the calm acceptance of personal tragedy that his stoicism demands.

Brutus shows generosity and kindness towards his servants and soldiers. With Lucius, he is ever patient and considerate, especially in the camp at Sardis. He has the comfort of his men in mind even in the midst of battle. At the end, he does not forget to express his gratitude to the last of his loyal followers, deeply thankful that he 'found no man but he was true to [him]'. It is this love for his men that inspires a reciprocal loyalty which endures until the bitter end. The remarks made by Lucilius and Strato testify to the absolute trust and confidence they have in their general.

In many ways, the play really traces the tragedy of Brutus, an honourable man, who becomes involved in an intrigue with less than honourable men and finds himself unable to deal with the consequences.

Mark Antony

In the first three acts, while Caesar takes centre stage, Antony is seen in the background, and has only a few lines to speak. Our first impressions of him are based on these and what the other characters say of him. Caesar shows a special fondness for him, and it is he who is to touch his wife to get rid of her 'sterile curse'. It is he whom Caesar turns to, to express his thoughts about Cassius. The 'gamesome' Antony is revealed as lacking the perceptiveness that Caesar has, when he refers to Cassius as a 'noble Roman, and well given'. This view of Antony as an innocuous presence in Caesar's shadow persists into Act II. Even Brutus thinks that Antony is 'but a limb of Caesar' and it has not been proved otherwise, so far. Only the deep-thinking Cassius is wary.

After Caesar is killed, we see him disappearing in panic from the scene of the assassination. But moments later, he is back, and from then onwards, he becomes a character to be reckoned with. He sends his servant with an obviously well-rehearsed speech, meant to flatter the conspirators and ensure his own safety [Act III, scene i, lines 126-137]. Already, we see a shrewd mind at work. Antony comes into the midst of the assassinators, fresh from their crime, but he has calculated the odds and is confident that Brutus' integrity will keep him safe. His grief is spontaneous and he makes no attempt to hide it [Act III, scene i, lines 148-150]. However, all his other moves appear planned to convince the conspirators that he presents no threat. He ignores Cassius' offer of power; he makes a glib expression of alliance [line 220]; he takes the hands of the conspirators in a symbolic gesture of friendship. All these, together with his unconcealed anguish, combine to establish Brutus' confidence in the conspirators' safety and Antony's support. So confident is Brutus, that when Antony asks to speak at Caesar's funeral, he willingly gives his permission. Only when he is left alone, does Antony reveal his rage at what he considers the most heinous crime of all and his sense of duty to a man he obviously idolized [lines 256-258]. The tearful, mourning Antony is infused with new strength and set on a deadly mission of vengeance.

Antony impresses us most with his shrewdness at Caesar's funeral, when he shows himself to be an accomplished actor, orator and politician. His appearance at the funeral also speaks much for his courage and confidence. He is courageous in facing a crowd that could easily turn on him, but he is confident of his ability to handle them. Antony has been thrust onto centre stage and he makes the most of his opportunity there. His understanding of the people and their susceptibility to the power of suggestion helps him to succeed. He begins on a humble and tentative note, but goes on to show that Caesar was not ambitious, with evidence that the people are familiar with [Act III, sc. ii, lines 83-92]. He refrains from openly contradicting Brutus as 'he is an honourable man' but scolds the crowd for not mourning Caesar. There is real anguish that he finds difficult to contain and he has to pause. However, the pause is also tactical, as he stops to assess how much the crowd has been moved by his speech thus far.

When he sees the people are sympathetic, he continues, encouraged. While pretending to abhor violence, he actually suggests it. When he sees that he has established a real connection, he baits the crowd further with the will, arousing their curiosity and greed. By this time, the people have turned against the conspirators, and the 'honourable men' have become 'traitors' and 'murderers'. Confident of their support, he goes down to them and shows them Caesar's bloody mantle. He works on their remorse and condemns the ring-leaders of the conspiracy, one by one, deliberating on Brutus' name, to remind them that Caesar was betrayed. While the people's remorse is at a height, he reveals Caesar's body, which is riddled with stab wounds. The people's immediate reaction is to seek revenge, but Antony holds them back. He tells them that he is not an orator like Brutus, who would stir them on to mutiny, thus pointing the direction for them to take. Antony stops them to read them the will because he wants to be doubly sure that the people are worked up into a frenzy so that there is no stopping them. Antony shows ruthlessness here, but it is the ruthlessness of a brilliant tactician pitted against a group of men who have just murdered 'the foremost man in Rome'. As a politician, Antony shows himself superior to Brutus, far shrewder and more in touch with reality and with the common people.

Antony's loyalty to Caesar, which makes him take on the role of Caesar's avenger, is impressive. Yet we have reservations about feeling total admiration for him. In quieter moments, we are disturbed by the unscrupulous aspect of his character. The cold-blooded manner with which names are ticked off for execution suggests callousness. His underhanded way of cutting off the people's legacy is dishonest, even if the money is not for his personal use but to pay the troops. Further, he shows treachery in his treatment of Lepidus, a member of the triumvirate, whom he likens to a beast of burden, who will relieve them of 'diverse slanderous loads' and 'groan and sweat under the business' until he can be stripped of power. His relationship with Octavius is very different. Octavius puts Antony's authority to the test at least three times in the play: when he differs in his opinion of Lepidus, when he points out that Antony was wrong in expecting Brutus to remain in the hills, when he disobeys Antony's direction to keep to the left hand of the field. Antony seems to be unable to control a younger but strong-willed fellow commander.

During the generals' parley, Antony holds his own against Brutus and Cassius. In fact, together with Octavius, he exudes much greater confidence and willingness to fight than his opponents. Later, his prowess on the battlefield is seen in his easy defeat of Cassius and his men. Towards the end of the play, Antony comes across as a more sympathetic character, one who recognises courage and loyalty. He is impressed with Lucilius and takes him into his service. However, this is also a strategic move. In the penultimate speech of the play, Antony pays a generous and moving tribute to Brutus, showing that he can be magnanimous in victory.

Cassius

In Act I, more of Cassius' flaws than any other characters' are revealed to the audience. Indeed, he comes across as a man full of envy, scheming to involve a man of honour in an assassination plot. His malice, his envy and his uncontrollable passion are clearly conveyed in the scenes where he tries to persuade Brutus and Casca to participate in the conspiracy.

In his speeches to Brutus, Cassius is unable to hide his feelings toward Caesar, who has attained god-like stature while he remains an underling. He has 'to bend his body if Caesar carelessly but nod on him'. He seems to be totally obsessed with this hatred of Caesar.

Cassius shows himself to be unscrupulous and will resort to dishonest means to achieve his ends. He writes the anonymous letters in 'several handwritings' to further persuade Brutus; he accepts bribes during the campaign; he has no qualms about suggesting the murder of Antony. All this seems to confirm the picture that Caesar paints of the envious person he is, 'Such men as he be never at heart's ease/Whiles they behold a greater than themselves.'

Yet, while these negative traits are the first things we notice, Cassius possesses qualities that Brutus lacks as a leader. He has a better understanding of human nature and is a far better judge of character than Brutus. He successfully persuades Brutus and Casca to join the conspiracy because he understands their characters and exploits their weaknesses. With the superstitious Casca, he makes use of the storm and the omens to get a promise of support. With the deep-thinking Brutus, he uses arguments and reasoning to win him over. Cassius is wary of the 'gamesome' Antony long before he reveals himself.

However, Cassius is never assertive enough with Brutus even when he needs to overrule his decisions. He questions Brutus' decision to allow Antony to live and to speak at Caesar's funeral but his doubts are brushed aside and he accepts this without protest. At Sardis, even though Cassius is a more experienced soldier, he accepts Brutus' battle plans over his own.

Throughout the play, Cassius is seen as a pessimist, filled with a sense of doom. This and his impulsiveness make him look to death as a way out. During the storm, on hearing that Caesar will be crowned, he tells Casca, he knows 'where [he] will wear this dagger' so that 'Cassius from bondage will deliver Cassius'.

This is not mere theatrics to impress Casca, as it happens again, in the quarrel with Brutus when in despair, he offers him his life. It is this pessimism, this eagerness to find his solution in death that precipitates his end. Titinius remarks that 'mistrust of [his] success has done this deed.'

As the play progresses, our impression of Cassius alters. We do not see him displaying the emotional outbursts that we see in Act I. In fact, in the quarrel scene, our sympathy tends to be more with Cassius, as Brutus seems to have abandoned his fortitude momentarily, and lashes out at him. Cassius is more subdued and more in control of his emotions. Although he makes some attempt to defend himself, he is incapable of matching Brutus' abusive tones. He shows himself more tolerant than Brutus and where Brutus has 'observed' and 'set in a note-book, learned and conned by rote' his faults, Cassius does not refer to Brutus' earlier mistakes. Cassius' deep affection for Brutus and his dependence on him lead him to endure Brutus' anger. In offering Brutus his heart to 'strike, as [he] didst Caesar', Cassius expresses real sadness, and his distress at the news of Portia's death is genuine. In this scene, Cassius' increased patience extends even to the meddlesome poet whom Brutus very rudely dismisses.

In his final appearances, Cassius shows himself courageous in battle, and ready to kill turncoats among his own troop. As with Brutus, he has loyal and respectful soldiers who stay with him right to the end. Titinius calls him 'the sun of Rome', for whose sake he will kill himself. Pindarus will trade his freedom to have Cassius alive. Brutus' regard for Cassius is summed up when he declares that he 'owe[s] more tears/To this dead man than you shall see [him] pay.'

While Cassius comes across as an embittered and vindictive man who is incapable of controlling his emotions in the first three acts of the play, the last two acts show him as a more sympathetic character, who probably deserves at least part of the glowing tributes his friends pay to him.

Casca

Of the minor characters, the most vividly drawn is Casca. He is seen as a treacherous man with no redeeming features. Casca is scornful of the common people and jealous of Caesar who he obsequiously serves in public but sneers at in private. It is clear how he regards Caesar's rejection of the crown when he remarks: '... he put it by once; but for all that, to my thinking, he would fain have had it.' However, his cynicism, is not without a basis, and probably indicates that he reads people better than Brutus does. Brutus considers Casca a 'blunt fellow' because of his appearance of simple-mindedness, but his hatred for Caesar is clear. Cassius, realising this, grasps the opportunity to win him over to the conspiracy. During the storm, in contrast to Cassius and Cicero who are unmoved by the omens, Casca shakes with fear. His superstitious and cowardly nature makes it easy for Cassius to extract Casca's promise of firm and lasting support with his own display of courage.

Cassius sees him as someone who can contribute to any 'bold or noble enterprise'. Yet, there is little that is bold or noble about Casca. His own base motives prompt him to observe that the conspiracy badly needs someone like Brutus to 'change [it] to virtue and to worthiness.' Casca is the first to strike Caesar and it is significant that his blow comes from the back, symbolizing his back-stabbing nature.

The shrewd Antony singles him out, together with Brutus and Cassius, when he condemns the conspirators in front of the crowd. His epithets for him range from the ironic 'valiant Casca' to 'the envious Casca' and finally to 'damned Casca'. The lasting impression we have of Casca is that of a small-minded, frustrated and insidious enemy of Caesar's.

Decius Brutus

Decius Brutus is in the conspiracy for very much the same reasons as Cassius and Casca — hatred and envy of Caesar. Despite his brief appearances in the play, Decius shows a remarkable understanding of Caesar's weakness. He first engages our attention when he offers to lure Caesar to the Capitol, during the conspirators' meeting at Brutus' house, as he claims he could 'give his humour the true bent' and ensure that he arrives at the Capital.

This boast proves itself when he exploits Caesar s susceptibility to flattery with his own interpretation of Calphurnia's dream. He understands how highly Caesar regards his own courage and when he insinuates that Caesar's absence may be interpreted as a sign of his fear, Caesar takes the bait. Decius also mentions that the Senate has decided to offer Caesar a crown, and this reveals how well he understands Caesar's ambition. Decius is treacherous and this is seen in the way he effectively hides his feelings in soothing words of concern to Caesar when he assures Caesar that his 'dear, dear love/To [his] proceeding' compels him to caution him about what he may lose if he does not go to the Capitol.

He is also the person who asks, 'Shall no man else be touch'd but only Caesar?'

Like Casca and Cassius, he is not averse to the idea of killing others who may threaten the conspiracy's success. His hard-headedness leads him to interrupt Brutus' And Cassius' jubilation after the murder and remind them what they should be doing.

Portia

As a wife, Portia has definite ideas about her role in marriage. It is not only to 'dwell in the suburbs' of Brutus' pleasure but to share the secrets that trouble her husband. She shows understanding and tolerance in the way she has borne her husband's strange behaviour without pressing him further, until the night of the conspirators' visit. Portia's fortitude is seen in her ability to endure her self - inflicted wound in silence. She uses this fact to persuade Brutus to unburden his secrets to her. Deeply moved by this, Brutus acknowledges Portia's virtues as a wife in his exclamation, 'O ye gods/Render me worthy of this noble wife!' Brutus and Portia, as seen in the only scene where they appear together, have an intimate relationship of mutual love and respect. This is obvious in the remarks each makes about the other.

In Portia's next appearance, much of her strength seems to have dissipated under the strain of Brutus' terrible secret. She is seen in a state of nervous anxiety, confusing Lucius with her instructions because her fortitude has abandoned her. One senses that Portia derives her strength from her husband. Thus, when they are separated because of Brutus' exile, Portia is unable to bear the news of Antony's and Octavius' growing strength, on her own. She becomes distracted with grief and takes her own life.

Despite two brief appearances in the play, Portia makes an impression onus. She is endowed with masculine strength, being Cato's daughter and Brutus'wife, but she is also very much a woman, capable of feeling fear and anxiety for her husband.

Calphurnia

At her first appearance, Calphurnia shows herself to be dominated by Caesar and she accepts his humiliating instructions to stand in Antony's way in silence. In fact, she only really speaks in the privacy of their home when her fears for her husband give her the courage to try to persuade him to stay at home. Caesar's manner to her, however, remains harsh and distant and he seems to be more concerned with declaring his courage than with her feelings. When Calphurnia goes on her knees, Caesar obliges her but his decision to stay at home is reversed by Decius' timely appearance.

Calphurnia has a complete trust in omens and is certain that her dream and the prodigies of the storm foretell her husband's doom as 'When beggars die, there are no comets seen/ The heavens themselves blaze forth the death of princes'. It is her love for Caesar that makes her risk incurring his annoyance by prevailing on him to give in to her premonition. While Calphurnia shows her love in this concern for Caesar's safety, there is no reciprocal affection on Caesar's part. There does not appear to be much of the husband-wife relationship in their marriage that we see in Brutus' and Portia's marriage.

Calphurnia contributes to the significance of the supernatural portents in the play as she is vocal in warning her husband. However, just as Caesar ignores the other signs, her warning goes unheeded.

The Common People

The common people appear in three important scenes of the play. In the opening scene, they are presented as a good-humoured lot, but easily influenced. The cobbler has his joke at the expense of Marullus and Flavius but he and the rest of the crowd are in turn scolded and made to feel guilty about celebrating Caesar's victory.

The crowd is not seen in the forum on the feast of the Lupercal, but reported on by Casca. Here Shakespeare shows them to be gullible, easily impressed by theatrical displays. They are completely taken in by Caesar's play theatrical performance. It is this impressionability that causes them to be moved by Antony's extravagant exhibition of grief and indignation at Caesar's funeral. While not stupid, the common people are uneducated, capable only of comprehending simple arguments and respond to emotional appeals. It is not surprising then that Brutus with his calm intellectual reasoning fails to reach them. Antony, on the other hand, employs graphic illustrations which the people can easily grasp. Their cries of 'Let him be Caesar!', and '... Caesar's better parts shall be crowned in Brutus' are a testimony of Brutus' failure. Their frenzied reactions at the end of Antony's speech show how effectively Antony has worked on their feelings, by exploiting their guilt, vanity and greed. The common people are seen at their worst in the senseless killing of Cinna the poet. They have been transformed by Antony's performance at the Forum into a mindless mob, set on inflicting violence on anyone they encounter.

ADDRESSING THE QUESTION

Read the question and underline the key words. Always follow the instructions in your question. For some exams, there may be two parts to the question. Some exams allow a choice of questions. The task may be clarified with words such as *show, explain, discuss, compare, describe, to what extent, what and how.* Think of the ideas you form from reading the context. Use these ideas in your answer. Where appropriate, comment on Shakespeare's use of language and/or literary devices to support these ideas. Think of the play as a whole and relate the importance of the context to it.

The formats of the questions below are varied. Some questions are similar to those in the GCSE and answers require a comment on the context as well as a response on an important aspect of the play as a whole. A few essay questions are not context based but still requires reference to the text in their answers. The samples provided are to show ONE way of responding to the question. There are thousands of acceptable answers and you are encouraged to develop your own insights into characters, events and the language Shakespeare uses. This can only be done by reading and analyzing the text carefully, several times, throughout your course. Remember the play has been tested in many examinations in many parts of the world for many years. Thus, the main components of the play, the themes, characterization and events discussed in many study guides may have some similarity. However, you, as a student, can add something fresh to your answer. If you are required to give a response to a context question, first you need to make the context real. What does this mean? The context will probably be familiar, but to add another dimension to your answer, look at it with fresh eyes. Engage with the context as you read it; imagine the scene before you as if you were there; articulate the sounds (not too loudly, if you are in an exam hall!), feel the emotion behind the words and respond. Do not forget to support your answer with evidence from the text. This is likely to impress examiners more than rehashing answers, including the ones in this book.

QUESTIONS & ANSWERS

Remember that the answers give <u>one</u> point of view. You may find information in the section on comments that may provide other relevant material.

SAMPLE QUESTION

1. In the opening street scene in Act I, scene i, two tribunes, Marullus and Flavius meet a group of tradesmen who are celebrating Caesar's recent victory over Pompey.

MARULLUS

You blocks, you stones, you worse than senseless things!
O you hard hearts, you cruel men of Rome,
Knew you not Pompey? Many a time and oft
Have you climbed up to walls and battlements,
To towers and windows; yea, to chimney tops,
Your infants in your arms, and there have sat
The live-long day, with patient expectation,
To see great Pompey pass the streets of Rome;
And when you saw his chariot but appear,
Have you not made an universal shout,
That Tiber trembled underneath her banks
To hear the replication of your sounds
Made in her concave shores?
And do you now put on your best attire?
And do you now cull out a holiday?
And do you now strew flowers in his way
That comes in triumph over Pompey's blood?
Be gone!
Run to your houses; fall upon your knees,
Pray to the gods to intermit the plague
That needs must light on this ingratitude.

Starting with this speech, explain how Shakespeare illustrates how persuasive speakers can influence others.   .

Write about:

- how Marullus' succeeds in dispersing the crowd in this speech

- how at least two of the following: Cassius, Marc Antony and Decius succeed in influencing their listener/s.

Plan

How Marullus succeeds:

- Rebukes crowd harshly →gets attention, evokes guilt
- Shows contempt for Caesar—repeats Pompey's name but not Caesar's →Caesar's unworthiness
- Uses rhetorical questions→ asserts the truth crowd cannot deny
- Angrily orders crowd to repent— celebration is wrong and punishable

How Antony and Decius succeed:

Antony

- Understanding of people → structure speech—contradicts Brutus without obviously blaming him
- Displays sorrow →wins sympathy
- Teases them with the will—further evidence of Caesar's generosity
- Shows Caesar's corpse →puts people in a frenzy

Decius

- Gives flattering interpretation of dream as good omen—Rome revitalized by Caesar →happy with explanation
- Mentions Senate planning to crown Caesar—works on his ambition
- Senate may change mind- risk of no crown →Caesar decides to go

SAMPLE ANSWER

In *Julius Caesar*, Shakespeare shows how important events are set in motion by powerful speeches either made to an individual or a group. In the above context, Marullus first rebukes the crowd for their disloyalty to Pompey with harsh epithets such as "blocks", "stones', "hard hearts" and "cruel men" to get their attention and to evoke guilt for so easily transferring their allegiance to Caesar, Pompey's conqueror. Marullus follows his first short rhetorical question ' Knew you not Caesar?' with another that is 10 lines long. In doing this, he is able to visually* and aurally* jolt the memory of the crowd by reminding the lengths they would go to just to get a glimpse of Caesar. This uninterrupted section also reflects the sustained anger that Marullus has to vocalise*. He repeats Pompey's name three times in this short speech, yet does not refer to Caesar by his name but as the one "That comes in triumph over Pompey's blood". In this way, his contempt for Caesar further emphasises Caesar's unworthiness. Immediately following this, he asks three beginning with "And do you now...", asserting the charges that the crowd cannot defend. Marullus highlights their fickleness and betrayal and fills them with further remorse. To conclude his outburst, he orders them to pray to avoid divine punishment for their "ingratitude", clearly stressing their celebration in the street is morally wrong. The crowd feels the impact of Marullus' indignation* and passion and moves silently away, abandoning the celebration. This display of the power of rhetoric* over the masses is introduced in the first scene to indicate the crucial part persuasive speech plays in manipulating people.

Just as Marullus succeeds in evoking guilt and shame among the common people in the street, Marc Antony is able to overturn the impact of Brutus' speech on them at Caesar's funeral with his oratorical skills. His understanding of the commoners' mentality helps him to structure his speech to exploit their weaknesses. Speaking after Brutus has left the scene, Antony subtly contradicts Brutus' claim that Caesar was ambitious by reminding the crowd that he had filled 'the general coffers', had 'wept' with the poor and 'did thrice refuse the crown', while carefully avoiding accusing the 'honourable men' of any wrong doing. He displays conspicuous sorrow for the dead Caesar and this wins the sympathy of the onlookers. Once he sees them softening, his speech gathers momentum*; he mentions 'mutiny', which he claims to be incapable of rousing. Antony further teases the crowd by mentioning Caesar's gift to them in his will, showing further evidence of his generosity. Finally, he works the people into a frenzy when he shows them Caesar's corpse. At this point, he reveals the details of the will and the people are ready to 'burn the traitors' house' and avenge Caesar's death.

While Decius is not seen to influence a crowd, he plays a key role in ensuring Caesar goes to the Capital. When he arrives at Caesar's house to accompany him, Caesar has just given in to Calphurnia's plea that he remains at home because of the unnatural happenings and a dream she had. However, playing on Caesar's pride and ambition, Decius provides a different interpretation, an enticement and a word of caution to Caesar. He appeals to Caesar's ego by telling him that it is 'a vision fair and fortunate' and that the dream signifies that Rome will be revitalized by him. Caesar is clearly pleased that he is seen as capable of this. Decius tempts him further by mentioning that the Senate will offer him a crown that day. However, they 'may change' their minds if he stays away because of his wife's dream. Not wanting to put the crowning at risk, Caesar decides to go to the Capitol. Thus, effective persuasion based on their knowledge of their listeners' weaknesses enables Antony and Decius to manipulate them.

SAMPLE QUESTION

2. Read the extract in question 1 above and answer the question which follows.

   Answer both part (a) and part (b)

a) How does this speech contribute to the opening of the play? Refer closely to details from the extract to support your answer.

Plan for (a)

- Arresting opening— angry tribunes versus celebrating crowd
- Introduces underlying conflict
- Highly charged speech— harsh epithets to rebuke crowd
- Mentions Pompey's name three times→ reminds them of him
- Describes vivid scenes → recapture their admiration for Pompey
- Rhetorical questions— assert indefensible charges
- Orders the crowd to atone for celebration—punishable sin
- Prepares audience for conflict and power play, role of easily manipulated people

SAMPLE ANSWER (a)

The play opens with the tribunes in a state of consternation* against a background of celebration. In the extract, Marullus is determined to disperse the crowd. His speech is important in revealing at this early stage the underlying conflict in Rome and the characteristics of the common people. Marullus begins by rebuking the crowd using harsh epithets: 'blocks', 'stones', 'worse than senseless things', 'hard hearts', 'cruel men of Rome', to express his anger and get their attention. He immediately mentions Pompey by name and does so three times in the short speech to remind the crowd of their erstwhile* hero and leader. He describes visually* and aurally* vivid scenes of how the people would scramble to catch a glimpse of Pompey. He reminds them how they would climb up 'to walls and battlements....to chimney tops' their 'infants in [their] arms' and make 'an universal shout' to jolt their memory and recapture their admiration for Pompey. Marullus expresses his outrage in the repetitive rhetorical* questions, 'And do you now....' which form a series of three accusations the people cannot answer. Finally, he orders them to atone for their sin, 'to intermit the plague'. This short speech is charged with emotion and we see the impact of Marullus' words when the crowd disperses in guilt and shame. It is appropriate that Shakespeare opens the play in this manner as it sets the emotional tone and prepares the audience for more scenes of conflict and power play. They are also given a view of how easily manipulated the common people are, and foreshadows the important role they play in Caesar's funeral scene.

(b) The unnatural happenings in the play affect people in different ways'. Show how reactions to these strange happenings reveal their beliefs and character. Refer to at least two characters in the play.

Plan for (b)

- How omens affect Caesar—disregards Calphurnia's warnings,
- Defiant to soothsayer, augurers
- Decision to stay at home because of wife's plea—but Decius flatters him into going to Capitol
- How omens affect Cassius—not alarmed like Casca, not superstitious
- Cassius' attitude to omens early in the play –uses them to recruit Casca
- How it changes towards the end of the play—begins to believe in signs—
- Eagles are replaced by ravens , crows and kites—instills expectation of imminent defeat

SAMPLE ANSWER (b)

In the play, several characters witness or are told about the omens and strange happenings. The soothsayer first warns Caesar of the Ides of March, but Caesar dismisses him as a 'dreamer'. Despite Caesar's dismissal of the omens, there are signs that he is superstitious. Before Calphurnia's appearance, Caesar had sent his servant to bring him the result of the sacrifice. When Caesar is told about the unnatural occurrences by his wife, he boasts that one look at his face could cause these 'threats' to disappear. Not wanting to show any vulnerability, he declares that no one can elude fate and that these are signs to the world in general. However, Calphurnia points out that '[w]hen beggars die there are no comets seen'. His arrogance is reflected when he ridicules cowards who 'die many times before their deaths' and shows the futility of worrying about dying, as death 'will come when it will come'. Caesar disregards the augurers' warning not to leave the house because the sacrificial animal had no heart, and chooses to interpret it as a sign of his cowardice if he stays away. However, he relents when Calphurnia goes on her knees to plead with him. Caesar shows ambivalence towards signs and omens because of his pride and ambition. When Decius arrives and gives a different interpretation to Calphurnia's vivid dream of his statue spouting blood and many a lusty Roman washing their hands in his blood, he scoffs at Calphurnia's fears. The lure of the crown trumps his uncertainty about the omens and he goes to the Capitol.

Cassius, an Epicurian, is not superstitious and uses the happenings on the night of the conspirators meeting to convince Casca that the heavens have sent these 'instruments of fear and warning' of Caesar's growing power. Cassius begins to believe in omens. On the way from Sardis he noticed two 'mighty eagles' which are birds of good omen, flying down to their 'foremost standard', where they perched and ate from the soldiers' hands. They accompanied the troops all the way to Philippi where they abandoned the army. In their place, 'ravens, crows and kites', all birds of ill omen, have arrived. These flying over the troops form a deathly shadow over them, looking down on the soldiers as if they are ready to die. These omens, occurring at a time when

Cassius has little confidence in their power to defeat the enemies, cause him to believe in them. He accepts them as a premonition of his and Brutus' eventual defeat.

SAMPLE QUESTION

3. The conspirators meet in Brutus' house. Brutus has asked for their hands to indicate their solidarity and Cassius suggests that they take an oath.

BRUTUS

No, not an oath. If not the face of men,
The sufferance of our souls, the time's abuse-
If these be motives weak, break off betimes,
And every man hence to his idle bed.
So let high-sighted tyranny range on
Till each man drop by lottery. But if these,
As I am sure they do, bear fire enough
To kindle cowards and to steel with valour
The melting spirits of women, then, countrymen,
What need we any spur but our own cause
To prick us to redress? What other bond
Than secret Romans that have spoke the word,
And will not palter? And what other oath
Than honesty to honesty engaged,
That this shall be, or we will fall for it?
Swear priest and cowards, and men cautelous,
Old feeble carrions and such suffering souls
That welcome wrongs. Unto bad causes swear
Such creatures as men doubt, but do not stain
The even virtue of our enterprise
Nor the insuppressive mettle of our spirits,
To think that our cause or our performance
Did need an oath, when every drop of blood
That every Roman bears, and nobly bears
Is guilty of a several bastardy
If he do break the smallest particle
Of any promise that hath passed from him.

Starting with this speech, explain how Shakespeare shows that Brutus' honourable principles are both a strength and a weakness in the play.

Write about

- how Shakespeare shows Brutus' sense of honour in this speech
- how in the play, Brutus' strengths and weaknesses are linked to his sense of honour.

Plan

- Brutus rejects Cassius' suggestion of an oath – the suffering of the people, the corruption should be strong enough to bind them to their cause.
- They are Romans— their word is as strong as an oath.
- Only untrustworthy people take oaths.
- An oath will stain the purity of their cause.
- A Roman who breaks even a small part of an oath is not a Roman
- Strengths
- His honour binds conspirators
- It prevents rash murders of others
- It inspires the loyalty of soldiers
- Weaknesses
- Blinds him to lack of honour in others
- Trusts Antony to keep to his word
- Thinks the commoners will appreciate his honour
- Underestimates Antony's unscrupulousness

SAMPLE ANSWER

Brutus' honourable principles allow him to lead the conspiracy and rid Rome of a tyrant, but they also cause his political downfall. The above speech illustrates the depth of Brutus' commitment to honourable beliefs and behaviour. He rejects Cassius' suggestion of an oath as he believes that a Roman's word is as strong as an oath. He considers the growing tyranny and repression of the people as strong reasons to act. As 'secret Romans that have spoke the word' the only oath they need is 'honesty to honesty engaged'. Only 'priests, cowards', 'men cautelous' and 'old feeble carrions' need oaths. To swear an oath at this point is to 'stain the even virtue' of their cause. Brutus' passionate adherence to these principles is based on his own noble character. As a man of great integrity and as a Roman, he truly expects his fellow conspirators to possess the same level of honour. Indeed, his idealistic view of Romans here leads him to declare that if a Roman breaks 'the smallest particle' of a promise, he 'is guilty of a several bastardy'.

Brutus' own sense of honour is a strong point because it unites the conspirators under his leadership. Also, it protects others from being rashly killed as Brutus firmly believes in sacrificing only the tyrant, Caesar. When Cassius suggests Antony be killed, Brutus asserts that their 'course will seem too bloody' as they should be known as 'purgers, not murderers'. His noble behaviour also ensures the loyalty of his soldiers right to the very end. However, it blinds him to the lack of honour in other men. His assumption that other people possess the same level of integrity is a weakness which ultimately leads to his downfall. First of all, he misreads the character of Antony 'a limb of Caesar' and he expects him to appreciate his motive for Caesar's killing. He allows him to speak at Caesar's funeral believing that Antony will not blame them, as he was instructed. When Brutus speaks to the commoners at the funeral, he expects them to believe him and support him because he is honourable. However, they fail to understand what he has achieved for them through his honour. Trusting Antony's word is probably the most serious mistake of Brutus' as he succeeds in getting the people to mutiny against the conspirators. Honour alone does not equip him to successfully deal with his situation. In several instances, it becomes the source of his weaknesses.

SAMPLE QUESTION

4. Answer both part (a) and part (b).

a) Read the extract in question 3.
How does Shakespeare show Brutus' passionate commitment to his cause? Refer closely to details from the extract to support your answer.

Plan for (a)

- Brutus' rejection of Cassius' suggestion
- Dismisses Cassius' suggestion of taking an oath—based on own commitment
- Believes in integrity of all Romans
- Convinced of need to prevent unjust acts by Caesar
- Strong emotion in his speech
- Only untrustworthy people need oaths— not Romans
- Those who break only a part of an oath are not Romans

SAMPLE ANSWER (a)

In this extract, Brutus dismisses Cassius' suggestion of an oath and proceeds to explain why in a highly charged, yet rational speech. His aversion to taking an oath is based on his own commitment to the noble cause of removing a tyrant to keep Romans free. He also believes in the integrity of every Roman. He reminds the group that without their action, 'high-sighted tyranny' will cause 'each man' to 'drop by lottery'. Brutus highlights the injustice under Caesar who will kill Romans at random. Shakespeare's use of sibilants* throughout the speech conveys the hissing effect of Brutus trying to contain his feelings in the middle of the night, for example, 'the sufferance of [their] souls, the times 'abuse,' 'secret Romans' linked 'honesty to honesty' and 'suffering souls'. With these descriptions, Brutus expresses his conviction, arousing similar feelings in the group. He urges the conspirators to carry out the task, without staining it with an oath. Indeed, he lists those who would require an oath as 'priest and cowards, and men cautelous,', 'old feeble carrions' and 'suffering souls' who 'welcome wrongs'. Clearly, he is contrasting these deceitful men to the conspirators with their virtuous 'enterprise' and 'the insuppressive mettle' of their spirits. His exhortation for them to commit to the cause without an oath reaches a climax at the end when he accuses Romans who 'break the smallest particle' of a promise of being guilty of 'bastardy'.

b) 'Although Mark Antony is victorious at the end of the play, it is Brutus that the audience sympathises with'. Show how Shakespeare portrays Brutus as a more sympathetic figure than Antony in the play.

Plan for (b)

- Antony's superiority over Brutus— better understanding of people, shrewd, far-sighted.
- Not admirable—callousness, dishonesty.
- Brutus—noble →struggles to justify Caesar's killing
- Determined not to kill any other
- Respect and love for wife
- Few unsympathetic moments— quarrel with Cassius
- Compassionate master
- Honour at the basis of character
- Seen in different roles—audience has more complete picture of him

SAMPLE ANSWER (b)

In many ways, Mark Antony is portrayed as a superior soldier and politician to Brutus in the play. However, despite these attributes, it is Brutus that the audience can relate to more and sympathise with as he is shown in his role, not only as a conspirator but as a man of great integrity, a loving husband and a compassionate master.

In his dealings with the conspirators after the murder of Julius Caesar, Mark Antony shows political shrewdness and far-sightedness. His speech at Caesar's funeral skillfully overturns the impact of Brutus' speech and again shows how much more he is in touch with the people and with reality. However, the audience is unlikely to applaud Antony's callousness* in dealing with his enemies and with Lepidus, and stealing from the people's endowment.

Brutus, on the other hand, wins the sympathy of the audience from the beginning. His noble frame of mind is seen in the way he struggles to justify the killing of Caesar in his soul-searching soliloquy. Only when he convinces himself that Caesar's ambition will make him 'run... to these extremities' does he see the morality of the murder and decide to 'kill him in the shell'. He is determined to shed no further blood and will not ' cut the head off, and then hack the limbs', unlike Antony who enthusiastically ticks off a list of names for execution. We see his respect and love for his 'true and honourable wife' contrasted with Caesar's patronising treatment of Calphurnia. If Brutus loses the sympathy of the audience, it is only momentarily. During the quarrel scene, for instance, he is at the height of self-righteousness. After berating Cassius unrelentingly, he proclaims that Cassius' threats are useless as he is 'armed so strong in honesty/That they pass by [him] as the idle wind'.

However, the abiding attribute that underlies most of his actions is honour. This is what maintains his connection with the audience. Even Antony himself recognizes this quality at the end of the play when he calls him 'the noblest Roman of them all'. As a husband, he shares a close relationship with Portia and shows the deep love and respect for his wife that are absent in Caesar and Calphurnia's interactions. Brutus' exclamation at the end of the intimate domestic scene, 'O ye gods/Render me worthy of this noble wife!' sums up his admiration for Portia. His words 'Portia is dead' at Sardis are poignant and evoke compassion in the audience. As a leader of soldiers, Brutus inspires those he commands and is consider ate towards them. Their loyalty at the end is best shown in Lucilius' willingness to be killed on his behalf. Brutus' more complete portrayal, showing both his weaknesses and strengths helps create greater audience sympathy for him.

SAMPLE QUESTION

5. Read the extract and answer the question.

The conspirators have just left Brutus' house and Portia, deeply concerned about her husband's frame of mind pleads with him to open up to her.

BRUTUS

Kneel not, gentle Portia. 278

PORTIA

I should not need, if you were gentle, Brutus.
Within the bond of marriage, tell me, Brutus,
Is it excepted I should know no secrets
That appertain to you? Am I yourself,

But, as it were, in sort, or limitation,
To keep with you at meals, comfort your bed,

And talk to you sometimes? Dwell I but in the suburbs
Of your good pleasure? If it be no more,

Portia is Brutus' harlot, not his wife.

BRUTUS

You are my true and honourable wife,
As dear to me as are the ruddy drops
That visit my sad heart.

PORTIA

If this were true, then should I know this secret.
I grant I am a woman-but withal
A woman that Lord Brutus took to wife.
I grant I am a woman, but withal,
A woman well-reputed, Cato's daughter.
Think you I am no stronger than my sex
Being so fathered, and so husbanded?
Tell me your counsels, I will not disclose them.
I have made strong proof of my constancy,
Giving myself a voluntary wound
Here, in the thigh. Can I bear that with patience,
And not my husband's secrets?

BRUTUS

O ye gods
Render me worthy of this noble wife! 304

Starting with this scene, explain how, despite their brief appearances, Shakespeare shows the important role of the women characters.

Write about

- how Shakespeare's shows the relationship between Brutus and Portia
- how Calphurnia and Portia contribute to the play.

Plan

- Portia is aware of Brutus' sleeplessness and anxiety.
- Portia wants to share his burden as his wife.
- She makes strong arguments to assure him she will keep his secret.
- Brutus is overwhelmed by admiration and love.
- His role as husband is another admirable aspect of Brutus' character.
- Calphurnia's relationship with Caesar – Calphurnia is deeply concerned –Caesar is patronising towards her fears
- Agrees to stay at home but changes mind when Decius re-interprets dream
- Caesar seen unsympathetic in his treatment of Calphurnia
- Calphurnia stresses role of omens in play

SAMPLE ANSWER

In the play, aspects of Brutus' and Caesar's character are revealed in the way they interact with their wives. The above scene is part of the only domestic setting that we see Brutus in and he shows himself to be a loving and respectful husband. While he says very little here, his reactions to Portia's speech reveals the depth of his feelings for her. Portia shows her cove and concern when she pleads to be allowed to share his burdensome secrets as his wife. Living outside the boundary of real married life, with all its problems, would make her his 'harlot' rather than his wife. Brutus is clearly moved and assures her that she is his true wife and as precious to him as his own blood. Portia further reminds him that Cato the general, was her father and she herself has given herself a wound and borne it in silence to prove her steadfastness. Clearly impressed, Brutus calls on the gods to make him worthy of her. The strong bond between Brutus and an equally stoical wife gives him added strength to stay on track in preparation for the assassination. Additionally, his sharing such a secret with her gives him some mental relief. Their relationship suggests an equal partnership with each partner contributing to the other's emotional well-being. However, this seemingly strong woman begins to lose her strength as the play progresses and finally commits suicide in the absence of her husband. Brutus' role as a husband is another admirable aspect of his character.

Caesar's relationship with Calphurnia contrasts with that of Brutus and Portia's. As with Portia, her appearances are brief. She is seen during the Caesar humiliates Calphurnia in public by asking Antony to touch her to cure her of her barrenness. At home, the interaction of husband and wife lacks the warmth and intimacy of that between Brutus and Portia. When Calphurnia begs Caesar to stay away from the Capital because of the unnatural occurrences, he first gives a defiant dismissal of death. However, Caesar eventually relents when Calphurnia goes on her knees. Her dream of Caesar's statue spouting blood is a fore-warning of his assassination, but when Decius gives a different interpretation of it, flattering Caesar, he changes his mind and decides to go. Caesar is seen as arrogant to his wife as he is in public, which makes the audience feel more alienated from Caesar's character. Calphurnia is an important voice in the series of voices warning Caesar. Her dream eerily reflects the manner of his death and adds importance to the role of the unnatural happenings in the play.

SAMPLE QUESTION

6. Read the extract in question 5.

Answer both part (a) and (b)

a) Look at how Brutus and Portia speak and behave here. What does it reveal about their relationship? Refer closely to details from the extract to support your answer.

Plan of (a)

- Brutus asks Portia to rise
- Portia challenges Brutus' love—questions her role in marraiage
- Appeals to his reason—she is his wife and Cato's daughter
- Reveals her self-inflicted wound—to show strength
- Brutus declares admiration and love
- Marriage between equals, deep love and understanding

SAMPLE ANSWER

Portia's kneeling clearly discomforts Brutus because he sees her as an equal not an inferior being, and he tenderly asks her to rise. Portia challenges his love for her in four rhetorical questions that would determine if she is his 'harlot' rather than his wife. Portia's need to know her husband's burden is based on her desire to support and help him as a wife. Brutus immediately confirms that she is his true wife as vital to him as his 'ruddy drops' of blood. Portia continues to press him to tell her his secret by continuing to appeal to his reason. She is more than just a wife and daughter, but Brutus' wife and Cato's daughter. On these two counts, '[b]eing so fathered, and so husbanded,' by two strong Roman stoics, she should possess more strength than a normal woman. She understands how her husband thinks and at this point, she succinctly sums up her request and assurance, 'Tell me your counsels, I will not disclose them'. Finally, she reveals the 'voluntary wound' 'in the thigh' that she has silently borne. This strikes a chord in the stoical Brutus and he is justly impressed. In the speeches, Brutus does not say much. He appears to be taken aback by Portia's display of love and strength. His remark at the end of her speech reflects his admiration and appreciation for his wife. Brutus and Portia clearly have a relationship based on deep love and understanding.

b) 'Cassius is more likeable at the end of the play than he is at the start'. Explain what happens to win the sympathy of the audience.

Plan of (b)

- At the start of the play, Cassius shows envious and dishonest nature—seen in the way he instigates and recruits conspirators especially how he succeeds with
- Brutus, including forging letters
- Underhanded
- Angry, weak and pessimistic—given to impulsive threats of suicide
- During the quarrel, Brutus expresses more rage and intolerance
- Real sadness at not being able to appease Brutus' anger—offers his life in real despair
- Shows sorrow and shock at Portia's death—empathy for Brutus
- Moving speech before battle—calm, resigned
- Fights and dies courageously

SAMPLE ANSWER

Cassius' appearance in Act I displays his envious and dishonest nature. His speeches to Casca and Brutus reveal his envy of a man with weaknesses who has grown so powerful that he must bow and bend before him. He is the instigator of the other conspirators and his unadmirable qualities are displayed in this role. His outbursts of anger often accompany his speeches to the conspirators. His underhandedness is seen in the way he recruits the conspirators, exploiting his knowledge of their characters. With Casca's superstitious nature, he interprets the signs as a warning about Caesar's growing power. With Brutus he arouses his sense of justice and aversion to tyranny. Cassius is unscrupulous enough to forge letters to persuade Brutus. In the first three acts, his highly-strung tendency alienates the audience as he seems weak and pessimistic and impulsively threatens suicide on occasions. However, he begins to gain more sympathy from the audience at Sardis. It is Brutus, who appears to be more emotional when he expresses his rage at Cassius. While Cassius attempts to defend himself with denials, he cannot match Brutus' barrage of accusations. When he offers his chest to Brutus to stab, there is real sadness and the audience is moved at this as Cassius appears to be in real despair. When he expresses shock and sorrow at Portia's death, there is genuine feeling. Indeed, he expresses more emotion than Brutus, here. The audience is given a glimpse of Cassius' empathy for Brutus. Before the battle, his sudden belief in omens signals his premonition of defeat and death. He notes the appearance of the 'ravens, crows and kites' in place of the eagles with a calm resignation. We see someone who is really preparing to meet his fate. He is composed compared to the other occasions when he speaks about dying. There is rapport between Cassius and his men who show their regard for him as a general. Cassius' act in freeing his slave, Pindarus, shows compassion, not seen in the earlier scenes. Cassius goes to battle as a general would, courageously, and meets his death as heroically as Brutus. The Cassius at the end of the play has redeemed himself and deserves the sympathy of the audience.

SAMPLE QUESTION

7. At the beginning of Act IV, Scene ii, the triumvirate is ticking the names of their enemies who are to be executed.

ANTONY

These many then shall die, their names are pricked.

OCTAVIUS

Your brother too must die. Consent you Lepidus?

LEPIDUS

I do consent-

OCTAVIUS

Prick him down Antony.

LEPIDUS

Upon condition Publius shall not live,
Who is your sister's son, Mark Antony.

ANTONY

He shall not live. Look, with a spot I damn him.
But Lepidus, go you to Caesar's house,
Fetch the will hither, and we shall determine
How to cut off some charge in legacies.

LEPIDUS

What, shall I find you here?

OCTAVIUS

Or here, or at the Capital.

ANTONY

This is a slight unmeritable man,
Meet to be sent on errands. Is it fit
The three-fold world divided, he should stand
One of the three to share it?

OCTAVIUS

So you thought him,
And took his voice who should be pricked to die
In our black sentence and proscription.

ANTONY

Octavius, I have seen more days than you,
And though we lay these honours on this man,
To ease ourselves of divers slanderous loads,
He shall but bear them as the ass bears gold,
To groan and sweat under the business,
Either led or driven, as we point the way,
And having brought our treasure where we will,
Then take we down his load and turn him off
Like to the empty ass, to shake his ears
And graze in commons. 26

Starting with this conversation, show how Shakespeare explores the pursuit of power in the play.

Write on:

- how Antony expresses his power in the above scene
- how the pursuit of power do not have similar endings for characters in the play.

Plan

- No deliberating, just marking names for execution
- Cold, callous—will kill anyone standing in way—tyrants bent on keeping power
- Shows extent mof ambition
- Expresses contempt for Lepidus
- Wants to get rid of him after using him
- Treacherous, wants to increase own share of power
- Needs to show superiority over Octavius

SAMPLE ANSWER

The triumvirate have assumed power after Caesar's death and they waste no time getting rid of their enemies. There is no deliberating or assessing the guilt of their enemies. Lepidus' brother and Antony's nephew are to be executed. Not only does Antony not object, he himself, coldly 'damn[s]' him with a 'spot'. The callousness of their actions suggest the three men are tyrants concerned with maintaining power at all costs. Antony, Caesar's avenger, is planning to kill not just the 'bloody men' who killed Caesar but anyone standing in his way, clearly showing the extent of his ambition. After he sends Lepidus away to fetch Caesar's will, he questions Lepidus' worthiness to share in their 'three-fold world' and sees him as a beast of burden to be disposed of after he is used. Antony's treachery here is clearly linked to his need to increase his own share of power. He is even patronizing to Octavius when he overrules his opinion to remind him that he is older and wiser than him. Octavius' status as Caesar's nephew appears to threaten Antony and he needs to display his superiority over the less experienced younger man.

The pursuit of power is most clearly seen in the actions of Caesar, Cassius, Brutus and Antony. Caesar's pursuit of power in the play is first seen in his defeat of Pompey. His foremost status is reflected in the crowd's celebration of his victory. When Caesar appears, his arrogant mannerism echoes Cassius' comparison of him to 'a Colossus'. He has ambition of being the supreme power in Rome and Brutus and Cassius strongly believe he will be crowned. This ambition causes him to ignore the many attempts to save him, ending with his ignominious death, stabbed from all directions by the conspirators in the Capitol. Cassius instigates the conspirators because of his envy of Caesar, a mere mortal, whom he believes does not deserve the power he has. Cassius is the chief instigator in the conspiracy and succeeds in influencing the conspirators to join. However, once Brutus is recruited, Cassius begins to play a secondary role. His influence is diminished once Brutus takes over as leader, and his opinions no longer prevail. At the beginning of the play, Brutus does not seek leadership. He has leadership thrust upon him. Because of his honourable nature and reputation, the conspiracy needs to be led by him. Once his position is acknowledged, he is confident and decisive, but he dislikes being contradicted and refuses to listen to advice. This leads him to make several mistakes, mainly, when he allows Antony to speak at Caesar's funeral and when he overrules Cassius' strategic suggestion on the battlefield. Both Cassius' and Brutus' pursuit of power ends in their deaths after they are defeated on the battlefield by Antony and Octavius' armies. Antony becomes Caesar's avenger and his power journey begins with the goal of bringing Caesar's murderers to justice. However, as part of the triumvirate, his action of getting rid of his enemies shows treachery and callousness. At this point, Antony seems to be on the same journey to absolute power as Caesar was. Unlike Cassius and Brutus, Antony's pursues power with clear political goals as he succeeds to rouse the people to mutiny and clear military goals which end with his victory over his enemies in battle.

SAMPLE QUESTION

8. Answer both questions (a) and (b)

(a) Read the extract in question 7.

What aspects of Antony's character are revealed in this scene? Refer closely to details from the extract to support your answer.

Plan of answer (a)

- Antony—callous —ambition cannot be obstructed
- Openly dishonest—intends using people's legacy
- Treacherous—will use Lepidus for his dirty work and then get rid of him
- Ambitious—not willing to share his power
- Threatened by Octavius— needs to dominate him

SAMPLE ANSWER (a)

Antony is seen to be callous and treacherous in this scene. The cold and impersonal way he marks the names of those who are to be executed suggests that he refuses to let anyone obstruct his ambition. Indeed, when Lepidus mentions his nephew Publius' name, Antony seems determined that his own nephew 'shall not live' and damns him 'with a spot'. He is open with his dishonesty as he reveals to his partners in crime that he intends using part of the people's 'legacy' that is left to them by Caesar. His treachery also extends to Lepidus, a member of the triumvirate. In his absence, Antony's shows how he is exploiting him like an ass carrying their 'treasure' to be sent to pasture when he has completed his task. His contempt for Lepidus is clearly seen in his dismissal of 'the slight, unmeritable man' and in his vivid and insulting comparison of Lepidus to the 'empty ass,' which will 'shake his ears/And graze in commons.' Antony's desire for greater power is reflected in his refusal to share '[T]he three-fold world' with Lepidus. Antony is seen to be domineering with Caesar's nephew Octavius when he suggests he is the wiser of the two as he has 'seen more days'. This suggests that Antony is somewhat threatened by Octavius and needs to remind him of his superiority over him. Later on, at the battlefield, this undercurrent of ill-feeling appears again, when Octavius refuses to keep to the left flank as Antony orders.

'(b) What does Brutus and Cassius' quarrel at Sardis reveal about their characters at this stage of the play?

Plan of answer (b)

- Strain of living in exile and coming battle
- A hostile Cassius appears, complaining about Brutus' punishment of his soldier
- Brutus tries to keep quarrel private
- He blames Cassius for defending a criminal and suggests that he himself
- is corrupt— mocking their cause
- Cassius is annoyed at Brutus being so strict with him
- Their bickering becomes childish at times, with personal insults
- Brutus is seen at his angriest moments, appearing to have abandoned his stoicism
- He is harsh in his criticisms of Cassius
- Cassius displays deep pain at Brutus' treatment of him and clearly shows his dependence on his love
- Unable to quell Brutus' anger at him, he gives him to despair and asks Brutus to kill him
- Brutus reconciles with him

SAMPLE ANSWER

In Act IV of the play, both Brutus and Cassius are showing the strain of living in exile and facing imminent battle. A hostile Cassius arrives in Brutus' camp and is asked by the latter to continue their talk in private, away from the soldiers. As a general, Brutus is trying to present to his soldiers, a united front between leaders. Cassius is angry that Brutus has punished his soldier, Lucius Pella, for taking bribes and ignoring his attempts to defend him. Brutus is direct in his counter and points out that Cassius should not have defended a criminal and that he, himself, is guilty of having an 'itching palm' and of having sold positions. Moreover, he tells him that he has escaped punishment only because of his rank. Brutus appears to be angered by Cassius' display of corruption which is fundamentally what the conspirators are against. He goes on to remind him that they killed Caesar for 'justice's sake' and for 'supporting robbers'; they would be tainting their just enterprise by accepting bribes. Brutus shows his constancy as he has not abandoned his principles despite the changed circumstances. Cassius expects Brutus to be more tolerant with him as he is a more experienced soldier and is more able to decide what should be done in these circumstances. Unlike Brutus, Cassius, who has never displayed the same strict moral code of conduct is not averse to bending the rules. They argue, momentarily appearing like squabbling children. Mocking and belittling Cassius for his 'testy humour', Brutus declares he intends to use him for his 'laughter' in future. Ironically, Brutus, himself, displays extreme hostility in this scene. His uncharacteristic angry outburst reaches a height and his remarks hurt Cassius, who expresses his disbelief. Cassius comments that even Caesar would not have dared to provoke him the way Brutus has and warns him that he may strike him if he continues in this vein. Brutus' self-righteousness reaches-a peak here, as he mocks Cassius by declaring that he is 'armed so strong in honesty' his threats 'pass by [him] as the idle wind'. Brutus accuses Cassius of turning down his request for money to pay his troops. At this point, Cassius gives in to despair and concludes that Brutus does not love him. He calls on Antony and Octavius to avenge themselves on him alone and offers his life to Brutus, who on seeing his distress, begins to console him. Cassius' emotional dependence on Brutus is clear and here, he appears to have given up hope without Brutus' support. Touched by Cassius' depth of sorrow, Brutus reconciles with him. The generals' quarrel is clearly mainly fuelled by the stress of the events leading to the impending battle. Later we learn that Brutus' unusual anger outburst is also due to the death of Portia, which he has to silently bear. This estrangement* between Brutus and Cassius is momentary and the two resolve their differences before the end of the scene.

SAMPLE QUESTION

9. In Act IV, Scene iii, towards the end of the quarrel between Brutus and Cassius at Sardis, Cassius expresses his sadness.

CASSIUS

He was but a fool that brought 84
My answer back. Brutus hath rived my heart.
A friend should bear his friend's infirmities,
But Brutus makes mine greater than they are.

BRUTUS

I do not, till you practise them on me.

CASSIUS

You love me not.

BRUTUS

I do not like your faults.

CASSIUS

A friendly eye could never see such faults.

BRUTUS

A flatterer's would not, though they do appear
As huge as high Olympus.

CASSIUS

Come Antony, and young Octavius come
Revenge yourselves alone on Cassius,
For Cassius is aweary of the world,
Hated by one he loves, braved by his brother,
Checked like a bondman, all his faults observed
Set in a note-book, learned, and conned by rote
To cast into my teeth. O, I could weep
My spirit from mine eyes. There is my dagger,
And here my naked breast: within, a heart
Dearer than Pluto's mine, richer than gold:
If that thou beest a Roman, take it forth.
I, that denied thee gold, will give my heart:
Strike as thou didst at Caesar. For I know,
When thou didst hate him worst, thou lovedst him better
Than ever thou lovedst Cassius. 107

Starting with this scene, explain how Shakespeare presents Cassius in the play.

Write on

- how the scene reveals Cassius' feelings
- how Cassius is a more sympathetic character towards the end of the play than he is at the beginning.

Plan

- Cassius denies accusations and is surprised and saddened at Brutus' intolerance
- Unable to appease Brutus' anger—only cold rebuttals
- Calls on Antony and Octavius to avenge Caesar on him alone
- Clearly hurt—calls on Antony and Octavius

- Alienated Brutus—hurts Cassius most
- More dependent on Brutus than Brutus on him
- Cassius envy and dishonesty shown in his recruitment of the conspirators
- Weak and impulsive
- Audience starts feeling sorry for him in the quarrel scene
- Bears the brunt of Brutus' anger
- Cassius incapable of defending himself
- Saddened by Brutus' attacks
- Offers his life
- Cassius is calmer. Not as emotional
- Belief in omen—does not affect resolve
- Brave in battle, compassionate to men
- Dies courageously

SAMPLE ANSWER

Just before this exchange, Brutus has accused Cassius of refusing to give him money to pay his troops. Cassius denies having done this and expresses extreme sadness that Brutus has magnified* his faults instead of overlooking them as a friend should. He is surprised and distressed that Brutus has not indulged him a little in this matter. Cassius is charged by Brutus and made to defend himself on being corrupted and tight with his money. After trying very hard to appease* Brutus's anger, Cassius receives cold rebuttals: Brutus does 'not like [his] faults; Cassius faults are '[as] huge as high Olympus'. Cassius' hurt is clear when he calls on their enemies to avenge themselves on him alone as he is tired of having his faults 'observed/Set in a note-book, learned and conned by rote'. While his speech suggests some self-pity, there is no denying that Cassius's sorrow is real. The fact that Brutus appears to be alienated* from him at this point is what causes him most anguish. It is evident that Cassius depends on Brutus' love much more than Brutus depends on his. His wanting to die is not something new. However, here, it does not sound like an impulsive reaction. Indeed, he sounds tired and resigned.

Our first impression of Cassius as an envious and dishonest conspirator against Caesar is confirmed by the way he recruits the other conspirators, especially Brutus. His resentment that a weak man has 'become a god' is clear in his lengthy account of Caesar's physical inadequacy to Brutus. His dishonesty is seen in the way he forges letters to ensure that Brutus is convinced that the people support him and are against Caesar. While Cassius comes across as perceptive, he seems too weak to uphold his opinion. Invariably, he gives in to Brutus whenever he contradicts him, for example, Brutus dismisses his warning of allowing Antony to speak at Caesar's funeral. We notice that Cassius is quick to threaten to kill himself, for example when he is told that Caesar will be crowned and when he thinks that the conspiracy has been discovered. From the quarrel at Sardis, Cassius becomes more a sympathetic character because of what he undergoes and how it affects his character. During the exchanges between the generals, Cassius bears the brunt of Brutus' anger. Cassius puts up a defence and engages Brutus in an argument. However, when Brutus continues to be relentless in his criticism of his faults, Cassius gives in to despair and again looks to death for release; however, it is not a reflexive act as in the earlier scenes. It appears more as if he has reached the end of his endurance. We find the emotional Cassius displaying a calmer attitude as the battle draws near. While he starts to notice signs, he does not allow his observation of the 'ravens, crow and kites' which have replaced the 'two mighty eagles' to weaken his resolve. With Brutus, he discusses how they will face defeat. There is a poignant moment when he concludes that 'this parting was well made', free from the histrionic*displays of the earlier scenes. He goes to battle bravely, befitting his status as a general. Cassius' treatment of his men and the release of his slave Pindarus show compassion that the audience has not seen in Cassius. While the audience is not surprised that he takes his own life, the manner with which he does it is probably more courageous than expected.

SAMPLE QUESTION

10. Answer both part (a) and part (b)

a) Read the extract in question 9.

What does it reveal to the audience of Cassius' emotional and mental state? Refer closely to details from the extract to support your answer.

Plan for answer (a)

- Cassius is upset – Brutus harshly counters every plea Cassius makes for leniency.
- Cassius is frustrated when he sees Brutus unwilling to show tolerance.
- Defensive but ineffective against Brutus' stronger charges
- Clearly very dependent on Brutus' good opinion of him
- Cassius gives in to despair—uses language to show he is the victim.
- Calls on Brutus to kill him as he killed Caesar—likely to make him feel guilty.

SAMPLE ANSWER

In Brutus' tent, the two generals continue their quarrel. Cassius has just been accused of refusing Brutus a sum of money he requested to pay his troops. Cassius denies this and attempts to placate* Brutus' anger by appealing to his friendship and tolerance of his faults. However, Brutus remains firm in his criticisms and counters every plea that Cassius makes for leniency. At this point, frustrated and beaten after Brutus' harsh rejoinders* to him, Cassius finally gives in to despair. He calls on Antony and Octavius to kill him as he does not see a reason to live, being treated so unkindly by the person he respects and loves most: '[h]ated by one he loves' and 'braved by his brother'. He acknowledges that Brutus is impervious* to his appeals, as he is '[h]ated', 'braved', 'checked' and his faults 'observed', '[s]et in a notebook, learned, conned by rote' . His use of numerous verb forms highlights the actions taken against him and shows him as a victim rather than a perpetrator*. Cassius clearly feels that he does not deserve Brutus' harsh treatment of his minor transgressions*. Brutus' alienation obviously hurts Cassius as he is clearly dependent on Brutus' love and good regard. To make up for what Brutus says he is guilty of, he offers him his heart, the ultimate sacrifice. Cassius brings Caesar up at the end of his speech to remind Brutus of the tyranny that he was so against. This is to emphasise how much more hatred towards him Brutus is showing at this moment. Cassius is clearly hoping to end the quarrel by making Brutus feel guilty.

b) 'Caesar's influence is more strongly felt after his death than when he was alive'. How is this shown in the play?

Plan for answer (b)

- Caesar dominates with his physical and political presence—evidence of his power and popularity.
- Struck down in most humiliating way—by his own senators.
- His murder sets in motion the course of revenge.
- Antony uses Caesar's body and his will to sway the crowd.
- Caesar is referred to by Brutus and Cassius – at Sardis and at their deaths.
- Caesar's ghost appears twice to Brutus.

SAMPLE ANSWER

Caesar appears in the first three acts of the play and in his appearances he dominates the scene with his physical presence. Characters defer* to him and flatter him. Crowds cheer him and he is offered the crown by Marc Antony three times. His speeches exude arrogance and power. Romans bend before him to petition redresses. However, at the height of his power, he is struck down in the most ignominious* way, stabbed from all directions. However, while he is no longer alive, after this moment, his influence is more greatly felt in the play. Indeed, Caesar's murder sets in motion the course of revenge. Antony is inflamed by the dead body of Caesar and swears to avenge his murder. During Caesar's funeral, Antony makes several references to him to remind the people of his generosity and uses his corpse to incite them to 'mutiny'. Caesar's influence is also reflected in the other characters' references to him. Brutus and Cassius mention Caesar in their quarrel. Brutus reminds Cassius that 'great Julius [bled] for justice' sake' and Cassius remarks that Caesar did not anger him as much when he was alive. Frustrated and despairing, he invites Brutus to '[s]trike as [he] did at Caesar'. Caesar's ghost visits Brutus twice, once at Sardis and once at Philippi to signal his impending*doom. Cassius dies addressing Caesar who is 'revenged/Even with the sword that killed [him].

Towards the end of the play, Brutus acknowledges Caesar's power when he sees the bodies of Cassius and Titinius and declares, 'O Julius Caesar, thou art mighty yet'. When he himself runs on his sword, he tells Caesar to 'now be still' suggesting that Caesar is finally avenged, nullifying* Brutus' futile* sacrifice. Caesar may have died in Act III, but his might is felt right to the end.

11. 'Omens and supernatural occurrences foreshadow important events in the play'. Show how Shakespeare uses them before the murder of Caesar, and the eventual defeat of Brutus and Cassius.

The occurrence of omens and strange happenings contributes to an atmosphere of disquiet and suspense in *Julius Caesar*. This would have a strong effect on the Elizabethan audience who were superstitious. Shakespeare uses them to indicate the immorality of the assassination and the approaching doom descending on Caesar, specifically, and the rest of Rome. Cassius' instigation of Brutus is immediately followed by the strange storm during which Casca observes 'all the sway of earth/Shakes like a thing unfirm'. This is accompanied by various strange signs, such as a 'tempest dropping fire', a common slave unharmed by his burning hand and a lion which passed by without hurting him. Besides these, Casca has seen 'a hundred ghastly women transformed with their fear' who swore they witnessed '[m]en, all in fire, walk up and down the streets'. The owl was seen sitting in the market place at mid-day, '[h]ooting and shrieking'. These strange phenomena* are witnessed by or told to several of the characters. However, they have different effects on them. Cassius, an Epicurian, is not superstitious and uses the happenings to convince Casca that the heavens have sent these 'instruments of fear and warning' of Caesar's growing power. Calphurnia believes they directly concern her husband as '[w]hen beggars die there are no comets seen'. These, especially her dream of Caesar's statue spouting blood and many a 'lusty Roman' bathing their hands in it, cause her to warn her husband to stay at home. However, Caesar chooses to ignore them and the augurers' warning of the heartless sacrificial animal because he could not appear weak and superstitious in front of the senate. Caesar also believes that fate cannot be avoided and death '[w]ill come when it will come'.

In addition to Brutus' and Cassius' growing lack of confidence before the battle, omens and supernatural warnings prepare the audience for their impending doom. The first supernatural sign is the appearance of Caesar's ghost at Sardis. While this could be a creation of Brutus' guilty mind, the Elizabethan audience would have accepted it as a supernatural warning of his defeat. Moreover, the ghost makes an appointment to see him again at Philippi, the battle site.

At Philippi, Cassius begins to believe in omens. On the way from Sardis, he noticed two 'mighty eagles' which are birds of good omen, flying down to their 'foremost standard', where they perched and ate from the soldiers' hands. They accompanied the troops all the way to Philippi where they abandoned the army. In their place, ravens, crows and kites, all birds of ill omen, have arrived. These flying over the troops form a deathly shadow over them, looking down on the soldiers as if they are ready to die. These omens, occurring at a time when Cassius has little confidence in their power to defeat the enemies, causes him to believe in them. He accepts them as a premonition* of his and Brutus' eventual defeat. All in all, the omens and the unnatural signs impose an unsettling mood of current and imminent disaster that the audience will find difficult to ignore.

12. 'Brutus' greatness rests on what he is rather than on what he does'. Show how far this is shown in the play.

As the play's main character, Brutus is depicted more fully than the other characters, including its titular character Julius Caesar. There is no denying that Brutus possesses many admirable qualities, such as honour, integrity, courage and compassion that earn him his status of greatness. However, his political naivete* and disregard for others' opinions lead him to act in erroneous ways that lead to disaster for him and his men.

From the outset, we are made aware of his honourable nature. Cassius needs him to lead the conspiracy because of his 'honourable mettle' and Casca acknowledges the public's regard of Brutus will change even wrong doings 'to virtue and to worthiness' with his leadership. Brutus' sincere stand against tyranny and its impact on free Romans leads him to justify the killing of Caesar as a political purge*and accept the leadership. At the conspirators' meeting in Brutus' house, the conspirators are attentive to his advice and forthcoming with their contributions. Metellus Cimber suggests the inclusion of Caius Ligarius; Decius volunteers to use flattery Caesar to draw him to the Capitol. What Brutus is, is sufficient to command the respect of the other conspirators. However, his integrity and nobility are tempered* with weaknesses in his character.

His sense of honour occasionally causes him to display self-righteousness, which reaches a height in his quarrel with Cassius at Sardis. While Brutus is inspirational to his followers, he appears to be alienated* from the common people and has little knowledge of how they think. More importantly, he is naïve in his assessment of Antony. Brutus' inflated* sense of self-esteem makes him incapable of accepting suggestions from others. Once proclaimed leader of the conspiracy, he expects his opinions to prevail over others'. This leads him to pursue a course of actions that causes him to commit serious errors which have disastrous consequences.

While Brutus is guilty of several errors, not everything he does deserves criticism. For example, Brutus' actions towards his wife show deep love and esteem, aspects which reflect greatness in a husband. He treats Portia as an equal and has high regard for her. In this aspect, he appears a more worthy husband than Caesar is to Calphurnia. As a master and general, he is kind and considerate towards his underlings, and inspires loyalty right to the end. This compassion for others is acknowledged by his men and they are willing to die for him. He faces his own death courageously, preferring to die under his own power rather than be humiliated by his enemy. These kind and brave actions stem from a noble character.

However, his actions as a leader ultimately lead to his defeat and death. Brutus ignores Cassius' advice on the threat that Antony poses; he allows Antony to speak at Caesar's funeral against Cassius' warning; he goes against Cassius' advice not to march to Phillipi. Finally, he makes a fatal strategic mistake by attacking Octavius too early, allowing Cassius troops to be overwhelmed by Antony's soldiers. Thus, it is Brutus' character which primarily displays his greatness and the audience is shown only a few glimpses of his greatness in his actions. Indeed, most of his actions appear to include serious errors which lead to his death.

13. 'Antony and Octavius are the instruments of justice in the punishment of murderers, but it is difficult to admire them.' Referring to the parts they play, explain why.

After the assassination of Caesar, Antony assumes the role of his avenger. Octavius, Caesar's nephew, arrives later to assume be his partner in bringing the murderers of his uncle to justice. However, Antony's scheming and manipulative ways warn the audience about his integrity. Antony's first act is to win the trust of the conspirators who are the perpetrators of this crime. Displaying caution and clever tactics, he sends his servant to ensure that it is safe for him to appear before them. On arriving at the scene of murder, he allows only sorrow and not rage to show in front of the conspirators. However, when he is alone with Caesar's body, his true feelings are expressed as he predicts 'domestic fury and fierce civil strife' will ensue as 'blood and destruction' prevail and 'infants [are] quartered'. It suggests that the intense rage that he feels will allow him to accomplish revenge at all costs, ignoring the accompanying damage that may be inflicted on Rome and Romans. This is in stark contrast to the spirit in which Brutus kills Caesar.

During Caesar's funeral, his manipulative speech turns the conspirators from 'honourable men' to 'murderers' and 'butchers', on a mission to destroy them all. Antony's unleashing of a mutinous mob in the streets of Rome will drive the conspirators out of Rome but he also begins the 'domestic fury'. The calculating way Antony achieves his end without regard to the impact on Rome is disquieting*. To Antony, the people are the tools of revenge that he exploits. Antony's strategy reflects his political savvy*, but it also shows his lack of integrity, where his word to Brutus means nothing.

The scene that reveals Antony and Octavius as wanton* punishers is when the triumvirate tick names off for execution. The cold and callous* way that Antony and Octavius mark relatives to be killed show their main concern is to get rid of threats to their position. Antony's treachery seen earlier with Brutus and with the crowd is highlighted here again. In Lepidus' absence, he reveals that he does not want to share the 'three-fold world' with him and intends to get rid of him like an ass 'to graze in commons' after he has been used. There is an undercurrent of animosity* between the Antony and Octavius, which again comes to light on the battlefield when Octavius deliberately contradicts Antony's order to go to the left flank. Antony and Octavius do not show the honourable characteristics of men acting to restore peace and justice but those of ambitious and callous tyrants who have little regard for others. At times, they appear childishly challenging each other's authority in the midst of serious tasks such as selecting victims for execution and implementing battle strategies. Although after the battle, Antony spares Lucilius' life and Octavius takes Brutus' men into his service, these are political moves. They recognize good soldiers and see the benefit of having them on their side. Although Octavius accords* Brutus a full military funeral and Antony proclaims him 'the noblest Roman of them all' at the end of the play, they do so with the knowledge that he is no longer a threat to them.

It is difficult for the audience to admire Antony and Octavius despite their mission because their dominant characteristics are their ambition and power lust. Lacking personal integrity and ignoring the principles of a free Rome, they appear to be an extension of Caesar's tyranny and not the solution to it.

14. 'How many times shall Caesar bleed in sport?' In your opinion why does *Julius Caesar* continue to be performed today? Support your answer with references to the play.

The titular character Julius Caesar is a well-known historical figure, not only to Shakespeare's audience, but also to modern audiences. Even with little knowledge of history, global audiences should be able to see parallels of Caesar in the figures of more recent dictators. Thus, relevance of content is one likely reason that audiences will be interested in the play.

Its continuing popularity is also explained by Shakespeare's depiction of interesting characters, from the noble Brutus, to the envious Cassius, to the ambitious Antony, who engage the audience in some very dramatic moments. The main characters display a degree of complexity and the audience cannot help but be caught up in their emotions and rhetoric. For example, Brutus' soliloquy before the killing of Caesar reveals the deep conflict of an honourable man who needs to justify it as a purging of an evil entity 'and think him as a serpent's egg [a]nd kill him in the shell', rather than a murder urged by personal motives. The quarrel between Brutus and Cassius at Sardis captures the fraught emotions of generals tested by exile and impending war. Even minor characters are memorable. Portia's and Calphurnia's brief appearances display powerful expressions of spousal* concern and add another dimension to their husband's character. Brutus' respect and admiration for his wife is in stark contrast to Caesar's patronizing* attitude towards his wife. Others, such as the cowardly Casca and the flattering Decius, are portrayed with individual idiosyncrasies*. We remember Casca as a cynical* and servile* conspirator who stabs Caesar in the back, literally. Decius' function is crucial in the plot and he ensures that Caesar goes to his death, literally. His way with words touches on another important point of interest of the play: powerful and memorable speeches.

There are several examples of rhetoric which would engage the audience's intellect and impress it. From the opening scene where Marullus rebukes the jubilant crowd and disperses it in guilt and shame, the audience is given a foretaste of what is to come. Antony's speech to rouse up the masses to mutiny reflects a skilful orator manipulating his audience as he turns the crowd's perception of the 'honourable' men to 'butchers' and 'murderers' in a single scene. His oration at Caesar's funeral is perhaps one of the most famous examples of manipulative speeches in drama. There are several instances of characters engaging in debate, in an attempt to make a point or win the listener over. Portia makes a strong argument to persuade Brutus to reveal his worries to her; Cassius and Brutus exchange insults at Sardis, over issues of corruption and tolerance before the battle; the generals' parley before the battle is a display of verbal challenges.

The play is also entertaining because of the variety of settings that could be presented on stage. From the clash of thunder of the stormy night 'dropping fire' and the lion and the gliding ghosts in the city to the clash of swords on the battle field, the play is visually and aurally entertaining. The murder of Caesar itself when it takes place is spectacular in its goriness.

This is a fast- moving play. The recruitment of conspirators is completed by Act II scene i. By Act III, scene i, Caesar is killed. There is little respite between the murder and Antony's arousal of the rioting commoners. Tension is maintained before Caesar's murder and intensified after his murder. This is a play structured to create anticipation and suspense, and engage the audience both at a visceral* and at an intellectual level. Thus, it is not surprising that Julius Caesar is still one of Shakespeare's most performed plays after all this time.

Glossary of words used in the sample answers

accords	gives
alienated	separated
animosity	hostility
appease	soothe
aurally	relating to sounds
callousness	cruelty
consternation	anxiety
cynical	distrustful
defer	give in
disquieting	disturbing
erstwhile	former
estrangement	division
futile	unsuccessful
idiosyncrasies	mannerism
ignominious	humiliating
impending	approaching
impervious	resistant
indignation	anger
inflated	exaggerated
naïveté	gullibility
nullifying	making useless
magnified	exaggerated
momentum	pace
patronizing	humiliating
phenomena	occurrences
placate	calm
purge	cleanse
premonition	forewarning
prevail	succeed
rejoinders	responses
respite	relief
savvy	knowledge
servile	very submissive
sibilants	the 's' or 'sh' sounds
spousal	relating to partners in marriage
tempered	moderated
transgressions	faults
visceral	primitive
visually	relating to sight
vocalize	speak
wanton	unrestrained

Other questions to consider and answer:

15 'Cassius was determined to have Brutus in the conspiracy right from the start'. Referring to the part Brutus plays, how far was Cassius wise in persuading him to join?

16. How does the meeting of the conspirators at the home of Brutus reveal the strengths and weaknesses of Brutus as a leader?

17. What impression do you get of the ordinary citizens of Rome in Act I, scene i? Explain how this is confirmed and how other characteristics are revealed later in the play.

18. 'Cassius, the conspirator is quite different from Cassius the soldier'. Explain how this is shown in the play.

19. How do the following contribute to the interest of the play?

a) Portia

b) Calphurnia

c) The Soothsayer

20. Explain why Brutus, rather than Antony, is considered to be the hero of the play.

Printed in Great Britain
by Amazon

59407385R00037